From the *Poorhouse* to the *Penthouse*

THE ULTIMATE SECRET TO RICHES

By Kay Haugen

Globalwide Publishing

THIRD EDITION PUBLISHED 2003

*From the Poorhouse
to the Penthouse*

Copyright © 2002
by Kay Haugen

Scripture quotations are from:
The Holy Bible
King James Version
Copyright © 1986 World Bible Publishers

PUBLISHED BY GLOBALWIDE PUBLISHING

ISBN: 0-9722360-0-7

COVER DESIGN AND LAYOUT BY KELLY MAXSON
ILLUSTRATIONS BY BILL ROBERSON

PRINTED IN THE USA

Kay Haugen came from meager beginnings. She spent her first years on a cotton farm located miles from town in West Texas. The family lived in a small frame house with a dirt yard that was frequently plagued by rattlesnakes. The living conditions in West Texas were hard: blistering heat in the summers and freezing cold winters, not to mention the sandstorms with their ninety-mile-per-hour winds.

The trials and tribulations of that hard country life were too much for Kay's mother, who had to be hospitalized for a mental breakdown when Kay was only three years of age. Throughout Kay's childhood her mother suffered with chronic depression and a debilitating sleep disorder known as narcolepsy. As a result of these illnesses, Kay's childhood vanished as she took on the adult chores of caring for the household.

During her years in school, Kay faced even more difficulties. She suffered from crippling shyness and a serious reading disability. Considered a misfit by her school-mates, she was shunned and brutally teased. The pressures both at home and school were at times too great for her; she remembers contemplating suicide as early as the age of twelve.

Later in life, in her mid-twenties there were even more challenges for her to bear. Kay was forced to take in her sick mother and care for her when her parents divorced. It wasn't long before the round-the-clock care for her mother took a devastating toll. After only six months, Kay's finances were exhausted. She and her mother were being evicted from her home, she'd lost her car, and her own health was deteriorating from the stress causing obesity, depression and a diagnosis of cancer. Once again her thoughts turned to suicide.

Finally, in her darkest hour, Kay met a total stranger, who upon hearing of her dire situation, gave her a collection of old, out of print spiritual books with the hopes of helping her. From these books and her Bible, Kay was able to piece together an extraordinary step-by-step process to access God's natural laws for the immediate attainment of prosperity, healing and happiness.

In one of the most phenomenal success stories ever recorded, Kay shares how she used this divinely inspired information to literally believe her way out of poverty, cancer, depression and obesity—into a multi-million dollar lifestyle, a svelte new figure, and glowing cancer-free health, all within an amazing 90-day time frame.

Over the years that followed, Kay began teaching others what she discovered. Eventually, the few classes she started teaching in her own living room grew into a multi-million dollar motivational seminar business. Through her business, she quickly developed a massive following that grew well into the thousands. After being asked numerous times by clients to produce a book that could be used to share her teachings with friends and relatives outside the country and in more rural areas, *From the Poorhouse to the Penthouse* was born.

This valuable little book holds a treasure trove of information that will catapult your chances for more success to the next level and take you beyond positive thinking, into the tangible, proven realm of limitless, instantaneous success in your finances, weight, health, sales, business and personal life—right now.

For best results, it's recommended that you read this book in its entirety, in the exact order the chapters are set forth.

CONTACT INFORMATION
If you have a success story you would like to share,
a question or would just like to say hello, I would love
to hear from you. E-mail KAYHAUGEN@SBCGLOBAL.NET

Signed,
Kay Haugen

Dear Gentle Reader,

You don't have to work as hard as you think you do to succeed. There are laws of nature which science does not yet fully understand—laws that can be tapped into and utilized by you to more rapidly and effortlessly accomplish the goals you dare to set for yourself, without limitations.

God's eternal laws regarding our beliefs and their effect on our reality are just as real as the law of gravity. Until these laws are fully understood and properly directed, they can just as surely take you down the path of destruction—as well as bless you beyond measure. I know this to be true, because I have experienced both outcomes.

In closing, it is my hope that this little book will inspire you to dream bigger than you ever have before and show you better ways to accomplish those dreams more quickly and easily than you could imagine.

Sincerely yours,

Kay Haugen

Pamper Yourself

This is one of those wonderful little books that you start reading and just can't put down. To fully embrace the promises of the abundant life this book holds for you, set aside a block of time for yourself, prepare yourself a lovely cup of tea or coffee, tune out the world and enjoy.

If you don't have an afternoon or evening to spare, then you can put this book on your nightstand or in your bathroom and read one or two chapters a day.

What a powerful difference this little book will make in your life, if you'll take the time to read it thoroughly from cover to cover!

A Special Thank You and Dedication

To the wonderful stranger who mysteriously appeared in my life back in 1984 and then suddenly disappeared before I could thank her. God bless you for caring enough to give me those incredible books, your act of kindness saved my life. You left before I could properly thank you, so I am thanking you now by dedicating *From the Poorhouse to the Penthouse* to you, because it was born of your loving example to care enough to pass the greatest secret on.

With eternal gratitude,

Kay Haugen

From the Poorhouse to the Penthouse

THE ULTIMATE SECRET TO RICHES

By Kay Haugen

TABLE OF CONTENTS

I

A WHOLE NEW WORLD
OF POSSIBILITIES AWAITS YOU!

For thousands of years, scientists, philosophers, and theologians have known that as part of our human makeup, there exists a vast reservoir of untapped potential.

Throughout history there have been numerous accounts of the unexplained, amazing demonstrations of super-human strength in emergencies as in the case of a person of normal size and stature lifting a car from a child, the fascinating musical talents of child prodigies and the inconceivable mathematical abilities of savants and autistics, similar to those portrayed by Dustin Hoffman in the movie "Rainman." There are also the astounding stories of miraculous healings and the little understood phenomenons of mental telepathy, telekinesis, bi-location, remote viewing, and the special spiritual gifts of prophecy, knowledge, tongues, and healing.

These facinating abilities have by their very existence *proven* that an infinitely higher realm of intelligence and possibility does exist for us. The important questions to now ask are, "Is there a way for the average person to readily tap into these higher realms of supernatural potential?" and "What is available for us there when we do?"

Welcome to an exciting new world of limitless possibilities that exists for us right here, right now. A new world of never before dreamed of possibilities, for healing, wealth, success, happiness and the perfect solutions to all of your problems that you can freely access at anytime you choose!

You are cordially invited to join the ranks of thousands who have already learned how to freely enter into this new dimension of extraordinary possibilities. These courageous pioneers, who have learned to think beyond the glass ceiling of limitation, have proven that the possibility to live beyond the common experiences of this world does exist. They have shown through a deeper wisdom, purity of spirit and much more advanced use of positively directed thought that it is possible to tap into limitless resources and radically alter your reality for the better, effectively causing positive circumstances to occur that would otherwise not have occurred and effortlessly attracting anything you want into your life without exception. As remarkable as this may seem, it is all true.

But quickly, before you start assuming that this is just another one of those self-help books that espouses the simple benefits of "positive thinking," you should know that this could not be further from the truth. This book will take you light years beyond the basics. It contains a plethora of brand new insights and critical elements to the creative process that have not yet been brought to light under the cover of one book and promises to take all those who are ready…to the next level.

By utilizing the new insights contained within this book along with the same thought energy you use every day, a new life of lifelong health, abundant wealth, the perfect job, your soulmate, limitless success in your business, effortless and permanent weight loss, the home of your dreams, love, beauty and endless good fortune, can all be drawn into your life and effortlessly laid at your feet in perfectly orchestrated ways that are a blessing to you and all concerned. Whatever life you can imagine or goals you would like to attain, no matter how impossible they may seem to you right now, will be possible for you to effortlessly attain with miraculous expediency.

Through a deeper wisdom, it is possible to cause circumstances to occur that would otherwise not have occurred.

This is not based on some sort of pollyanna optimism or wishful thinking, it is based on proven and sound scientific facts—facts that *also*, interestingly enough, correlate perfectly with biblical scriptures. But as real as this all is, sadly many will miss out. Why? Because they're unwilling to venture into new and uncharted territory and believe that more is possible than what they have experienced. Opting instead to hold on to only what is familiar and comfortable, even if that means robbing themselves of a new life full of extraordinary possibilities and continuing to go on living their lives of insufficiency, sickness, turmoil, loneliness and unhappiness. They are satisfied with the status quo, happy instead to go on living in their familiar realm of knowledge and mediocre possibilities.

By not being open to the possibilities one can literally cost themselves a lifetime of undreamed of benefits and blessings

Whenever I encounter people like this, I *implore* them to at least try the new concepts, "If you'll be willing to open your mind and take the time to put what is being proposed here to a test, the results will absolutely confirm everything! Think of it, won't it be great to live the life of your dreams in overflowing health, wealth, love, success and happiness, with enough abundance left over at the end of the day to help those who are less fortunate in the world?" and a typical response will be, "That all sounds well and good, but I don't have the time to deal with that right now!" Again, an attitude that is indicative of someone who isn't willing to step outside their comfort zone of familiar experience.

But, given the sheer gravity and magnitude of what is actually being promised here, one has to consider this type of closed-minded attitude to be most unwise...most unwise indeed! Whatever the problem, whether it be a busy schedule, laziness, fear of the unknown, false pride and arrogance in one's own abilities, satisfaction with the status quo, disbelief or just plain old fashioned hard-headedness...by all counts no excuse will really suffice. Please pardon my candor here, but a mind that isn't open to investigating such massively beneficial possibilities, especially when there is no cost whatsoever involved in testing and proving the validity of the concepts for oneself, is a mind that is far *too* closed.

By not being open to exploring the possibilities one can literally cost themselves a lifetime of undreamed of benefits and blessings, not only for them, but also for many, many others. So, it's not just about ourselves! It is about the collective blessings we could all be, to not only those who are closest to us, but to the millions of others in the world who are in desperate need (approximately 1.1 billion are now living in extreme poverty worldwide), and a waste of valuable resources on this enormous scale is too great.

The Bible says, "Let your light shine before men, that they may see your good works (do good in the world) and glorify your Father which is in heaven." (Matthew 5:16) This scripture explains that when you let your light shine and do good works that you are actually honoring and pleasing your Father. So, why continue to hide your light or shrink away from being all that you can be that is good in the world? Whether you are religious or not, it makes no sense whatsoever for you to do so, because when you do you're of absolutely no good to yourself or others. Many feel a proud sense of spiritual piety when they live a minimal existence and they wear their piety like a badge. They profess things like, "I have what I need to get by and that is enough!" and "Money is not important to me!" This is because no one ever taught them that their Heavenly Father actually *wants* His children to prosper exceedingly from His boundless supply and for very good reasons! Because,

> *If you want to achieve phenomenal success in uncommon hours, you must be willing to take the time to learn more about the special mental work that is required for its attainment.*

when we do and then use that money to purchase goods and services and invest, over and above what we first tithe and give to charity, that it is actually just *additional ways* of blessing and supporting others.

In reality, by prospering exceedingly, living below your means, giving generously, putting some into investments and being a good consumer, you are not only blessing the poor in the world, you are also blessing the entire chain of people who are associated with all those goods, services and investments with jobs, security, medical care, food, housing and educational opportunities for their children—thus, keeping them out of poverty! As an example, when you so much as purchase a pair of jeans, you are blessing and supporting everyone down the line, from the person who sold you the jeans to the farmer who grew the cotton! The bottom line is this…the more you prosper…the

more you can give, invest and responsibly spend (in order of importance)…and the more people you can bless and support in this world!

The Lord does want you to prosper and live a good life, regardless
of what you may have been taught. Don't forget that Abraham, who
was one of our Father's favorites, prospered exceedingly and had the
very best that life had to offer and He wants the same for you!
"Beloved, I wish *above all things* that thou mayest prosper and be in
health, even (at the same level but not beyond) as thy soul prospereth
(a soul prospering in the ways of righteousness,
goodness, love, clean living and charity that is
only full of the best intentions for good in the
world)." (III John 1:2)

*Why continue to work harder
when you can work so much
smarter and with so much more
efficiency and effectiveness?*

So, regardless of what your parents, society,
your peers or your church may have told you,
just re-read the words in these two scriptures, take them to heart, and
know that you're *supposed* to let your light shine by prospering, being in
health and blessing others to whatever extent that you can! So, don't
hold back for another moment, start being all you can be right now.
You'll be doing yourself and the world a huge favor when you do!

The vast majority work hard all of their lives but their lives don't
ever really change; they diet but they don't lose weight, they seek good
health but never attain it, they want more money but don't ever get it,
they work on their relationships but they don't improve, they want better jobs but don't get them, they desire to travel but never do, they seek
their soul mates but don't find them, they want more business but don't
attain it, and they dream but their dreams don't come true. By these
examples one can clearly see that most people do desire a better life,
but history has already proven that desire and effort alone are not
enough to make that happen. No, if you want to achieve phenomenal
success in uncommon hours, you must be willing to take the time to
learn more about the *special mental work* that is required for its attainment.

The most common mistake people make regarding the achievement
of their goals is to think that the accomplishment of the daily tasks
required to achieve them is all that is necessary. Fact is, if you do not

first take the time to do the special mental work needed to firmly imprint a new foundation for success deep within your mind, true and lasting success will not be a possibility for you, *no matter how hard you work*. This is an inescapable truth according to a law (more on this particular law later) that is as concrete and inflexible as the law of gravity.

Unfortunately, if the proper mental foundation for success is not first established in your mind, each and every time you try to succeed you will be blocked and sabotaged at every turn; you will lose weight and gain it back, you will get ahead in your finances and experience setback after setback each time that you do, you will find new business deals and opportunities but they won't come through for you. All highlighting the fact, that until you change on the inside…you cannot change on the outside.

The images you love and give physicality through your senses in the invisible realm and continuously believe will come to pass, will become real in the physical world. They have to because it is the law.

However, once the new mental foundations for the successes you want to achieve with your weight, health, finances, relationships, business, etc., are properly established and *combined* with the other steps that are necessary, the changes you desire will all take place easily, naturally and permanently. Everything that you need to attain lasting success will effortlessly fall into place for you; new circumstances will be drawn into your life for the highly-accelerated accomplishment of your dreams!

I like to tell people this, "If highly unusual events are not happening for you on a daily basis to help you realize your goals and dreams in a time-frame that is well outside the norm…then you're not doing it right!

If this is what is actually possible for you, then the question you need to ask yourself is this, "Why should I continue to work harder when I can work so much smarter and with so much more efficiency and effectiveness?" This is a chance for you to actually live your dreams and to make a real positive difference in this world! Don't let it slip through your fingers. Seize the opportunity and get ready for the time of your life!

To exemplify what is possible with the right mental foundation for success, are several well-known self-made multi-millionaires/billionaires who have achieved phenomenal success in their lifetimes, and these highly esteemed individuals are: Donald Trump (the famed real estate mogul), Oprah Winfrey (multi-media mogul, beloved talk show host and accomplished actress), Bill Gates (founder of Microsoft), Dexter Yeager (legendary Amway distributor), Jim Carrey (one of Hollywood's highest paid actors), Mary Kay Ash (founder of Mary Kay), Lance Armstrong (seven time Tour de France champion and cancer survivor), Muhammad Ali (world champion boxer), Tiger Woods (one of the top golfers of all time), and Sam Walton (the founder of Wal-Mart).

These high achievers have one characteristic they all share in common, regardless of whether it was a learned skill or they came by it naturally, they are all "habitual forward thinkers." Meaning, that they've all developed the persistent habit of positively imaging themselves living and enjoying the lives they wanted as if they were an already accomplished fact, *before* those fantastic lives ever happened. Many books espouse the power of mental imagery, but then leave out key ingredients needed to give the imagery real creative power.

Here are a couple of those important keys (more keys will be shared later); while they imaged what they wanted to achieve in life, they would also hold the same feelings (joy, excitement, success and love), along with the appropriate physical sensations (touch, taste, smell and hearing) that would be associated with those images as if they were already real. It was the ceaseless repetitions of this "type" of mental imaging that actually formed the mental foundations that were needed for their successes. Then once the mental foundations were formed, they would relentlessly believe, through all adversities, that their images would come to pass.

To put it more simply, they first produced the vivid mental images of the success they wanted in life and then they *loved* and *physically connected* with what they were seeing. Then, once the proper mental foundations were formed they *relentlessly believed* (had undaunted faith) their dreams would become reality. Here is a very special insight for you…love is the emotion that gives a vision its highest creative power.

In fact, since the very beginning, all creation has happened through the emotion of love. Love is the purest conduit for the creative process. But, it is your physical sensations of touch, taste, smell and sound and the undaunted belief in the realization of your goals, that builds the bridge necessary for the images you are holding in the invisible realm to cross over into the visible realm. In summation, the images you love and give physicality through your senses in the invisible realm and continuously believe will come to pass, will become real in the physical world. They have to because it is the law.

The imagination is where all mental foundations for success are initially formed before they ever become reality. As a matter of fact, nothing great in life has ever been achieved without its emotionalized mental equivalent first being established in the fertile creative field of someone's mind. This would include everything from winning the Olympic gold, to building a sky scraper, going to the moon, the development of computers and the internet, and even the smallest things you see around you, the cars, art, clothes and furnishings. Everything had its first beginnings in someone's imagination. All things were lovingly designed and created first in the invisible realm before they ever became visible. The most elementary basics of the creative process are; first the mental equivalent….then the corresponding emotional and tactile (touch, smells, taste and sound) connection with the mental equivalent…now the relentless belief in the realization of the mental equivalent…then the right words and actions (more on these important aspects later)…and finally the physical reality. How important is it to have a vision? The Bible says, "Where there is no vision, the people perish…"(Proverbs 29:18) Evidently, it is extremely important!

Of course, not everyone is interested in achieving the same level of success as these super achievers, but you can be assured that if you were, it is entirely possible. You can develop the same mental skills and tap into the same incredible resource (more on this best kept secret just ahead) that these people have, if you only have the desire and are willing to take the time.

II

THE BEST KEPT SECRET

People come from a variety of backgrounds including the purely scientific, the spiritual types, the devoutly religious, the deep thinkers, the philosophers and everything in between. Regardless of a person's background, education is universally important and when new information comes to light that could be of benefit to us, it is always worthy of investigation. For those of us who trust ourselves to make intelligent decisions, the fear of exploring anything new does not exist because we know we always have the option to reject anything we choose.

Are you ready to know what the best kept secret of all time is? I'll bet you are, right? I mean who wouldn't want to know that? Well, let me tell you that the best kept secret of all time is not out there somewhere over the rainbow, it's not a fountain of youth, or a magic pot of gold waiting to be discovered. The best kept secret of all time actually exists in the last place you would probably ever look for it. It exists inside of you!

Within you, at the core of your being, is an infinite resource more vast and powerful than anything your mind can presently fathom. And once you learn how to properly tap into it, this incredible resource has the endless capacity to solve any problem you have and make you as rich, loved, happy, fit, healthy, and successful as you would like to be with no limitations in the blink of an eye! I know that at first pass this may sound too far-fetched to be believed…but it is absolutely true and is important information that should definitely not be ignored.

This little known resource that resides within you, has not only been proven to exist scientifically, but has also been clearly spoken of in the

Bible, as will be examined more closely later. This resource within you is a pure stream of limitless possibility that continually pours forth from the very core of your being. It is a raw, creative source, connected to limitless resources, whose sole purpose is to create every single aspect of the reality you experience.

This creative process has been tirelessly and impersonally carried out throughout the course of your life. This massively complex operation has been continually directed to create according to the countless number of varied thoughts, belief patterns and images, both the positive and the negative, you have provided to it as it flowed through your mind—basically turning you into your own "human reality factory."

The creative process, which takes place below your conscious level of awareness, is so vast and complex that it is beyond the normal person's ability to conceive; exhibiting the incomprehensible ability to simultaneously orchestrate every move of every person on the surface of planet earth. Determining when, if and how our paths will cross and for what specific purposes that will happen for when they do...for good, bad or indifferent.

This leaves absolutely nothing that happens in any of our lives to chance, coincidence or accident, it all happens by design...designs we are each responsible for providing. A very quick and simple way to test this creative process is to first pick a random target goal; it could be a particular color and model of car, a certain type of bird, a particular color shirt, up-front parking places, new clients, more phone orders, etc.

For those who have been seeking and are ready to know the truth, nothing will keep them from making that discovery.

Now picture what you want to attract very clearly in your mind and then boldly repeat, "I *now* attract an unusual abundance of (fill in the blank) or "I am a magnet for (fill in the blank)." Don't forget to image what you want, *as* you repeat your affirmations and do this several times over and wait and see what happens. You will soon see results! Thus, proving to yourself beyond all question the creative connection between mind and reality.

This highly individualized creative process finally offers a rational explanation as to why our lives turn out so differently, why our paths all take such varied directions, why some turn out to be so fortunate in life while others are not so fortunate, and why bad things happen to good people. It is all being determined by the specific mental directives that we each provide every step of the way.

As was commonly thought, when bad things happen to us it is not because we're being punished. No, in reality we have unintentionally brought these things upon ourselves. You are now and always have been the one who is responsible for the reality you experience, and in light of this interesting fact, you *also* have the power to change your direction at any time your choose! Once you become familiar with the limitless attributes of this great resource within you, and learn how to fully tap into it, and more consciously and positively direct it, any life you can dream of having will be possible for you to quickly attain. Any life at all…without exception. The truth is the only limitations you have are those that you place on yourself!

A mind once stretched by a new idea, never regains its original dimensions.

For the scientific perspective on this phenomenal internal resource, we can look to the study of quantum physics. In quantum physics, the pure, raw, reality generating energy that is flowing from within you is referred to as the "quanta."

The quanta, like all things in the universe, is made up of energy that is vibrating at a certain frequency. The frequency at which the quanta vibrates is nature's most pristine and harmonious—the most perfect level of vibration possible.

We are also vibrating, with our personal frequencies being determined by the fluxing states of our individualized consciousnesses. When we stray from perfect alignment with the relaxed, evenly modulated frequencies of the quanta which are those of perfection, peace, unconditional love, right living, faith and harmony and enter into the highly disruptive frequencies of fear, lack, worry, stress, hatred, criticism, anger, guilt, sin, doubt, unforgiveness, etc., we throw our frequency out of alignment with the quanta and drastically restrict the flow of infinite possibilities that are available to us.

You are a conduit through which the quanta or pure, boundless, raw possibility flows and your degree of access is determined by your degree of alignment with the perfect frequency of the quanta.

The Chinese have known about this internal resource for over five thousand years and refer to it as your "Chi" or life force energy. As a special point of interest, I once witnessed a Chinese Chi Gong healing master, who is a master of directing the Chi or quanta, direct that power to heal a woman's bladder tumor instantaneously, "live," as it happened on ultrasound. Let me tell you, it is easy to believe that more is possible when you actually see a tumor gradually shrink and then disappear completely right before your very eyes!

The same qualities of the quanta and Chi have also been echoed to exist in the Hindu faith. In the Hindu faith this omnipotent resource within is referred to as the Jiv. The Jiv is the divine which exists at the core of one's being. Looking at all of the world's major religions there exists a common thread which connects them all to one another, including the Christian faith, which shall be examined more closely later.

You know, they say that fiction often imitates real life and I think that's true. For example, could the reason that movies like Star Wars, Superman, the Wizard of Oz and Peter Pan have all become so beloved be because on a deeper level we all knew there was a grain of truth to the amazing possibilities they represented for us?

Upon closer observation of Star Wars for example, the higher power they referred to as "the force," just so happens to represent the very same qualities of the quanta. The force, for those of you who didn't see the movie, was a higher power that the Jedi Knights (the good guys), through highly specialized training and their spiritual purity, could access for special powers such as levitation, mind reading, and other special skills that they used for good. Then there is Dorothy in the Wizard of Oz, who went to the great and powerful Oz to plea for help getting home, only to find out that she had the power to get home within herself all along. Or how about Peter Pan, who told the children to think a happy thought and they would be able to fly. See any correlation between your state of mind and accessing higher powers? Incredibly, like the movies, we are now discovering that more is possible for us as human beings than we ever previously imagined.

The quanta that flows from within you is an artesian spring of all knowledge, wisdom, perfect solutions, answers to all of the unanswered questions, supernatural healings, endless possibilities, lifelong health, limitless wealth, perfect guidance, love, joy, peace, harmony and materiality that is readily available to you, once you learn how to tap into it through the correct alignment of your frequency with that of the quanta.

What is possible for you when perfect alignment is attained? To answer this, we can look to the person who attained the full measure of potential that is possible through perfect alignment, and who was the first great teacher of these concepts, and that person is none other than…Jesus Christ. Are you a little shocked to learn that Jesus originally taught these same concepts? I know I was! (More on why His *original* teachings were altered later.)

Now, regardless of a person's religious background, most major religions and historians of the world do believe that Jesus did actually exist and that he did perform many miracles. They just don't agree on the definition of who He was. Some think that He was just an ordinary man, some believe He was the son of God (my personal belief) and others believe He was only a prophet. Regardless of what a person believes, by comparison to others throughout history, He has proven Himself to be the highest example of possibility (please forgive my boldness if you are of another belief), clearly demonstrating more supernatural possibility than anyone ever has before or since Him.

Jesus, who lived in perfect alignment, was a perfect conduit for limitless possibility and divine knowledge to flow through, exhibiting the omnipotent power to supercede all of the other natural laws. During His ministry on earth, through His perfect alignment Christ demonstrated the ability to materialize form, exampled by the multiplication of the fishes and the loaves, and the ability to transmute matter, as shown when He turned water into wine, raised the dead, healed the sick, calmed the storms, walked on water and overcame death. He also demonstrated higher divine knowledge, with the ability to read minds and foresee into the future, forecasting every detail of His own death and subsequent resurrection.

Possibilities are only limited by one's ability to believe.

Jesus was and is the highest example of what is possible for all of us. But, is everything Jesus did actually possible for you? Many think that it is not and they are absolutely right. But they're not right because it isn't possible! They're right because they don't *believe* it is possible. You see, because it is our own personal belief parameters *along* with our degree of alignment that determines the degree of what is and isn't possible for us, if they don't *believe* it's possible, then it won't be possible for them. This means that the more aligned you are and the bigger your belief parameters become—the more will be possible for you in your realm of reality. Therefore, if you will expand your belief parameters to the full measure and properly align yourself, nothing will be impossible for you. "If thou canst believe, all things are possible to him that believeth." (Mark 9:23) and "No good thing will he withhold from them who walk uprightly (those who live rightly or in alignment)." (Psalms 84:11)

To further show just how important your personal belief/faith parameters are, would be the fact that even Jesus, the most accomplished Master ever documented to exist throughout all history, could not perform miracles on those who did not believe! "And He did not many mighty works there because of their unbelief." (Matthew 13:58) And when miracles did occur, He was always quick to tell the people that the miracles happened according to their belief or faith. "Daughter be of good comfort; *thy faith* hath made thee whole." (Matthew 9:22) "Go thy way; *as thou hast believed*, so it be done unto thee." (Matthew 8:13) These scriptures make it abundantly clear, that it was their faith that was the "door" or "key" that made their miracles possible. Without their faith the miracles were not possible! The bottom line is this; the mighty power of God can only work for you if it can work through you, through the door that you open through your belief or faith.

"The power of God can only work for you if it can work through you"

God's limitless power is flowing from within you and the degree of that flow, limited versus unlimited, is purely determined by your degrees of alignment and belief. It is possible for you to dive-in right now and start swimming freely in the incredible sea of abundance where all things are possible, if you will only start to walk in alignment, believe without limits, claim the abundance that is already yours and begin to denounce all your fears of lack and loss and all of the other lower emotions that have been choking off the limitless power of God that flows from within you!

Regardless of what you may have previously believed about yourself or what you may have been taught, what Jesus did is possible for you according to the scriptures. "He that believeth on me (those who believe and follow what Jesus taught us), the works that I do he shall do also; and greater works than these shall he do…" (John 14:12) But why haven't we progressed any further in our abilities to tap-in and utilize this incredible resource? Because we have not had all the pieces to the puzzle. Tragically, those important pieces were lost over two thousand years ago for interesting reasons that will also be explained later.

Through my own discovery and utilization of the seven hidden secrets I found encoded in the Bible in 1984, I was able to calibrate my consciousness to the proper frequency and make a supernatural quantum leap in reality that forever changed my life and my perception of it. In this quantum leap, I was catapulted from a reality where I was penniless, jobless, overweight, sick with cancer, had no car, was dealing with an eviction, and all while taking care of my sick mother, into a new abundant life of overflowing health, wealth and happiness. Everything that I asked for on a long, specific list of needs and desires for me and my mother just showed up with supernatural expediency! A few of the seventy-two seemingly impossible goals that effortlessly came true in rapid-fire succession included, the instantaneous healing of my cancer, an astounding weight loss of seventy pounds in ten weeks, a new beautiful home with every specific amenity I had asked for, the perfect new job, a new car, an end to my financial problems with more than enough, a cure for my mother, and many joyous times for my mother and myself.

Starting from day one using the seven secret encoded teachings, one supernatural event after another was being perfectly orchestrated to lay my new life at my feet in the perfect ways, order and highly accelerated timeframe. Circumstances I could have never previously imagined as even being possible, fell into place perfectly like dominoes. This all happened automatically and there was no doubt that it happened deliberately, not by mere coincidence.

As far as the general concept of coincidences goes, there were far too many strange events occurring in rapid succession for me to consider any part of what was happening to be a coincidence. The incredible series of perfect alignments that occurred concretely validated for me the fact that there is really no such thing as a coincidence…no such thing at all! It was all clearly happening by design. In fact, I even made up a couple of new terms that I used to replace the term coincidence and those two terms were, "Godoinces" and "divine synchronicities."

The infinite creative power within had constructed a new reality for me according to a long, specific list of seemingly impossible goals I had made for myself and my mother, and did so perfectly with miraculous expediency. I successfully tapped into the wellspring and so can you, like me and the thousands before you who already have! But in order for you to be able to do this, you cannot be half-hearted in your commitment to apply the seven secret encoded teachings of Jesus. Your commitment must be total. In the famous words of Master Yoda, from the movie *Star Wars*:

> *"Try not. Do or do not!"* —*Master Yoda*

III

∽

THE MOST IMPORTANT CHOICE
YOU WILL EVER MAKE

Once you make your all-important decision to proceed ahead, a decision that only you can make, and learn how to properly tap into your God-given resource, a whole new world of possibilities will be available to you.

Remember when we were kids and we would pretend that we had a magic lamp with the genie who could grant us three wishes? While playing this fun game we didn't put any limits on our wishes, did we? That's because there were no limits to the possibilities that were available through this whimsical character, right? Well, there are also no limitations for the wellspring of infinite possibilities that exists within you. You can think of it like having your own personal Genie or Santa within! In fact, I think that these fictional characters were unknowingly created to represent the infinite possibilities that were given to you by your Father!

This was our Father's original design that He created for us, but the knowledge of its basic structure, function, limitless provision and directions for access were lost. In the absence of this critical knowledge, we have been living in a spiritual dark ages of sorts, experiencing all manners of unnecessary pain, illness, lack and suffering with no idea that the perfect solutions to all of our problems and needs has always been easily within our reach.

But the dark days we have been living in are soon to be over. Because the truth about the God-given wellspring within and our ability to access it is finally coming out, and this book's all-important purpose is to help that process take place on a much larger and more accelerated scale.

This is no ordinary book. Not only is it designed to impart to you the most valuable truths you could ever learn, which thrills me to no end by the way, but to also be a ready resource that can easily be passed on to others you know who are going through difficult times or who have the ambition to achieve more in their life and don't yet know the best way to get there. This powerful resource reveals to us all a new level of possibilities that we never previously imagined existed and provides seven extraordinary steps that have proven themselves to be a guaranteed way to turn any situation around and achieve any level of success a person wants to achieve.

> *This is no ordinary book, it was written to impart the most valuable truths in existence into the world.*

Believe me…the truths this special book contains within its' pages can make all the difference in the world to those who are open and willing to put them into application! I happen to know first hand, because this knowledge certainly made all the difference to me.

I will never forget how important and timely this information was for me when I was going through my darkest of times. When I think back on the incredible life I would have missed out on if that wonderful girl hadn't passed this information on to me, I cringe! Not only did it save my life, but it gave my mother a life she wouldn't have otherwise had. Beyond that, it has now given thousands of others incredible lives that I want for everyone! (The inspiring story of my meeting this girl, the full details of the devastating trials I was going through, the amazing miracles that followed and how I came to discover the seven remarkable steps that helped me to attain them will be shared later on.)

Think about it, because of just one person's loving, sharing heart, literally thousands upon thousands of people have already been blessed in positive ways. And with the rate this book is being shared that number will soon be in the millions. I wish that sweet girl, who was a total stranger to me at the time, only knew that what she did for me has ended up blessing so many people! She was a very important link in a chain of reaching others. It just goes to show that one person *can* make a big difference, even if they don't know it!

This book was created to carry on that girl's wonderful spirit of sharing and to be an effective tool to help to put an end to the pain in the world and spread more happiness, health, light, love, hope, inspiration, possibility and prosperity everywhere. But to continue to accomplish this lofty mission, I will need the help of all those who are willing to be another link in the chain. This is an open invitation for you to join in, if your heart guides you to do so, in the mission to reach those who would benefit from this information that has been hidden from us for so long.

The Starfish Story

Once upon a time there was a little girl on the beach picking-up starfishes that had become beached by the thousands (those who are unaware of the truth) and saving them one by one by picking them up and tossing them back into the sea (awakening them to their ability to access the limitless wellspring within). A group of children gathered on the boardwalk to point and laugh at the little girl's futile efforts. All except for one little boy, that is, who went down to the beach to ask her if she really thought she was going to be able to save all of the starfishes? She said to the little boy, as she chunked the one she had in her hand into the sea, "Maybe not, but at least I saved that one!" The little boy pondered what she said for a moment and then he started to join in and then one by one the other children up on the boardwalk joined in as well! They laughed and they played, until something really wonderful happened—they ran out of starfishes!

The moral to this story is that when enough people are willing to get involved to help reach others, enormous numbers of people can ultimately be blessed.

When you finish this book, if you feel it was truly beneficial to you and decide you want to be another link in that chain, it's easy. Check with the people you think would benifit from reading it, tell them how much the book benefited you and then either show them your copy or send them to the web-site www.fromthepoorhousetothepenthouse.com. Make a list of all those who want to purchase a copy (the larger the order the greater the discount) and place an order for your group using the toll-free number in the back of the book. "Starfish" cases starting at three to over a hundred (for large companies, churches, clubs, sports teams, charities, networking groups and multi-level marketing organizations) are available. When your case arrives, invite everyone to meet for coffee and deliver their books!

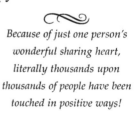

Because of just one person's wonderful sharing heart, literally thousands upon thousands of people have been touched in positive ways!

By taking the time to get this book into the hands of your friends you are actually providing them with a gift that will continue to bless them for life. The old saying goes, "Give a man a fish and you feed him for the day, teach him to fish and you feed him for life." *From the Poorhouse to the Penthouse* is like handing them the fishing pole and the tackle box!

But, I must warn you to be prepared because, not everyone is going to be receptive or interested in this information no matter how beneficial you believe its value to be. But why is this, you ask?

The reason is simple, in order to attain advanced spiritual enlightenment, a person must first be spiritually ready to receive that knowledge. And until a soul is ready to receive that knowledge they will be deaf, dumb and blind to the truth, even if you were to put it on a silver platter, put an apple in its mouth and put it right in front of them! "And the light (the truth of the infinite wellspring within) shineth in the darkness and the darkness comprehended it not." (John 1:5)

In Mark 4:3-20 we are told that sharing the truth is like sowing seeds. This scripture explains that not all of the seeds of truth are going to land on fertile soil! Some of the seeds are going to land in the weeds and on the rocks where they cannot take root. This would infer that some people who hear the truth will not be ready to accept it or believe it, because either their pre-existing erroneous spiritual beliefs (the weeds) or their hard heads and hearts (the rocks) will prevent it. We like to refer to these types as the "rock heads" (not to their faces of course!). Because no matter how badly you want to reach them with the truth, it is only deflected by their unreceptive, misinformed and disinterested minds.

But once a person has reached a point that they have enough of the light of God/Goodness in their hearts (an absolute requirement) and they have matured to the appropriate spiritual level (something that is not necessarily determined by regular church attendance or Bible knowledge), something wonderful happens! Their level of interest in knowing and applying the truth is radically increased and a "truth-detector" is activated within them that automatically recognizes the truth whenever it is encountered! Some of your previously held erroneous beliefs might try to tell you otherwise, but deep inside you will just know that you know. It is an unmistakable inner-knowing given to you by God!

Turns out that how a person responds to this book can be a very good way to test a person's level of spiritual maturity. For example, if you refer a copy to them and they find that once they've started reading it that they can't put it down, their soul is full of light and they are ready to progress ahead to the higher levels of spiritual enlightenment. However, if they won't read it at all or start to read it and then put it down and don't get back to it, they are…well, most likely the opposite of what I just said and are probably not yet ready to advance (unless of course, they are already highly accomplished masters who are in no need of further education!).

Operating with free will, some of us simply choose to progress ahead spiritually faster than others. I have worked with literally thousands over the years and some of the *least* spiritually developed people also turned out to be the most confident and accomplished in their careers, finances and materiality! But at the same time they were totally bankrupt in their relationships and had no detectable level of love in their hearts for others, which of course is the most important thing of all!

Because they were spiritually deficient, they lacked compassion and empathy for the feelings, lives and hardships of others, they always selfishly put themselves and their priorities first and wrongly considered money and things to be more important than people. Can you think of anyone you know who fits this description? Unfortunately these people, because their prosperity surpasses the prosperity of their soul, are prospering outside the will of the Father. Which results in prosperity that comes with a price, the price of happiness, peace, security and healthy relationships.

These self-serving narcissistic types, merely use people as if they were meaningless "pawns" that were put here for their own benefit, entertainment, service and pleasure and never really emotionally connect with them. Most of the time, the only person they ever end up caring about is themselves and many sadly find themselves alone. This type of self-directed, emotional vacuum effectively prevents these people from *ever* being able to develop long-lasting, happy, healthy, loving relationships.

A simple rule of thumb to follow to avoid this pitfall would be… always treat others the way you would want to be treated if you were in their shoes. Or the smart ones will eventually wise-up and move on (unless they happen to be extraordinarily kind or serious doormats that is)! And the truly sad thing with these poor narcissists is that they have no idea what an incredible life they're missing out on by remaining emotionally detached and spiritually bankrupt.

But don't let the lack of interest that these unfortunate souls have in their spiritual advancement hinder your progress in any way. Let them go and then show them what is possible by your own example! Trying to force them to believe as you do will only serve to push them further away anyway!

LEVELS OF SPIRITUAL MATURITY:

LEVEL ONE: *Eagle Egg* - a person who is not ready to accept the knowledge of the limitless resource within or the truth that our thoughts and beliefs are directly responsible for shaping all our circumstances for better or worse.

LEVEL TWO: *Fertile Egg* - a person who has been fertilized with the truth and has not rejected it, but is not yet ready to investigate it any further.

LEVEL THREE: *Hatchling* - the stage when the individual becomes interested and begins to feed vigorously on information through multiple books and seminars on the topic. Usually in this level the individual is only interested in learning more, but is not yet ready to apply that knowledge. Unfortunately some never advance beyond this stage.

LEVEL FOUR: *The Eaglet* - this is when the person has gained sufficient knowledge and is now interested in beginning to test and apply that knowledge in small ways.

LEVEL FIVE: *Fledgling* - at this point the individual is starting to build strength in their wings through more consistent application. They are beginning to see intermittent results from the occasional focus of their thoughts and beliefs. Their ability to focus and believe is still weak at this stage.

LEVEL SIX: *Young Eagle* - at this point the person has received sufficient proof that our thoughts and beliefs are directly responsible for shaping our circumstances for better or worse and all doubt of this truth is now fully resolved. Realizing this, they now begin to practice focusing more and more on the positive. But their application is still only intermittent, it is not yet daily. The success rate at this level is usually only about 30% - 50%, which, of course, is directly related to their consistency and ratio of limited vs. unlimited and positive vs. negative thoughts and beliefs regarding the outcome. The results can be either partially achieved goals or a "sometimes chickens, sometimes feathers" effect.

LEVEL SEVEN: *Eagle* - now the true mastery begins through the "daily" disciplined focus of one's thoughts and beliefs toward unlimited positive outcomes 50%-75% of the time. The positive results achieved at this level are now more precise and consistent than ever before with numerous miraculous breakthroughs. To attain and maintain this level one must focus every day. Inconsistency will throw you back to a level six.

LEVEL EIGHT: *Golden Eagle* - daily focus time has become a way of life and negative limiting thoughts have almost completely ceased to exist now, leaving unlimited positive thoughts and beliefs 75% - 99% of the time. Miracles are a very common occurrence at this level.

LEVEL NINE: *Platinum Eagle* - complete perfection, no limiting beliefs, only unlimited positive thoughts 100% of the time. The only one this writer believes has made it to this level is Jesus Christ.

What level are you now? What level would you like to achieve? The constant call to grow spiritually comes from deep within. It is that gentle urge inside of you that is always prodding you to advance toward perfection, harmony, improvement, balance, spiritual maturity, and to always make the right choices verses the wrong ones. The opportunity to submit yourself to that call is always readily available, but you also have free will.

We are the only creatures on earth that have the free will to either answer that call to progress toward perfection and advancement or to hang-up on that call and rebel. Many people live out their whole lives in rebellion and never do advance spiritually! But the opportunity to advance is always there for us.

If you have made your all-important decision to proceed, congratulations! Now it's time for you to start asking yourself what you really want at this point in your life! If you could design any life for yourself that would not only be a blessing for you, but a blessing for others as well, what would your new life without limits look like? If you could make a quantum leap from where you are right now into any new wonderful life of your choosing, what would you choose if nothing were impossible?

• If you are unmarried, you can choose to find your soul mate…the right person for a blissfully happy relationship. A marriage filled with love, happiness and joy.

• If your business is in trouble, you can choose the perfect solutions, people and resources to turn it around and create lasting prosperity and success.

• If you have been experiencing financial difficulties and debt, you can choose immediate miraculous financial increase…an abundance of money to meet and exceed your every need right now.

• If you are in poor health, you can choose to be totally healed and live in vibrant health for the rest of your life.

• If you live in fear, you can choose divine protection for yourself and those you love…so that no harm can come to you or them.

• If you are unhappy with your work, you can ask to be directed to your "perfect work"…where you will be fulfilled financially and emotionally.

• If you are unhappy in a relationship, you can ask for it to be either divinely healed or peacefully dissolved…whichever is for the highest good.

• If you live in cramped, dark conditions, you can choose a beautiful home filled with light. You decide if it is to be the little house on the hill or the big mansion by the ocean.

• If you are lost spiritually, you will ask for divine guidance in all spiritual matters.

• If you have unfulfilling friendships, you can choose to have new, quality friends, with an abundance of wonderful time to spend together.

No matter what you may have previously been taught or have believed, your Heavenly Father never wanted you to go without in any area of your life, whether it be spiritual, financial, health, love, happiness, companionship or otherwise; a truth punctuated by the fact that He *already* provided you with limitless provision when He created you. "Fear not little flock; for it is your Father's *good pleasure* to give you the kingdom (access to the limitless wellspring within through alignment)." (Luke 12:32) "Beloved, I wish above *all things* that thou mayest prosper and be in health, even as thy soul prospereth." (III John 1:2)

But if these scriptures are true, then why does the Bible *also* say that it would be easier for a camel to pass through the eye of a needle than it would be for a rich man to enter into the kingdom of heaven? Does that mean that it's wrong for us to prosper? Although this is what this scripture appears to say, it is not what it is saying at all!

In this scripture, the "rich man" represents someone who holds on too tightly to what he has, because he is afraid if he loses it he will not be able to replace it. In the kingdom of heaven, which is a consciousness of limitless, endless abundance, no fear of loss exists!

When you enter into the kingdom of heaven, you leave your fear of loss and lack behind at the gate and gain upon entrance the new assured confidence that through your faith you can always readily replace whatever is lost from the vast abundance within and are therefore never afraid to release that which you have.

By definition, the kingdom of heaven is the conscious awareness of the endless abundance that is readily available to you and your total confidence in your faith to call it forth at will.

Jesus lived in the kingdom of heaven right here on earth and so can you! Even though Jesus never carried anything with Him, He was the wealthiest man who ever lived! Through His perfect alignment and faith He was capable of calling forth anything He needed from the wellspring at any moment. Think of it, He turned water into wine and multiplied the fishes and loaves and told you that you can do the same! This means that you are capable of calling anything you want or need into existence at will. "I sent you to reap that whereon ye bestowed no labor…" (John 4:38) This is who you really are and what you are truly capable of (regardless of what you may have previously been taught), if you will only walk in alignment, accept the abundance that is already yours and learn how to believe with your whole heart.

But, I must warn you, until you have matured spiritually and have built your faith up, you should not release too freely that which you have or your lesson will be an easy one!

Also, while you're asking, always be sure to ask for more than you need so that you will have enough to generously share with others. As you grow and mature spiritually, your needs will all naturally be met and you will then start to become more selfless and interested in helping to care for others. Selflessness (which is the opposite of selfishness) is one of the great earmarks of a person who is reaching the higher levels of spiritual evolvement.

There are many people out there in the world who are totally dependent upon the kindness and charity of others, such as the disabled, the poor, the ignorant, orphans, the mentally ill, the sick, the elderly and the mentally retarded. These people are dependent upon the resources that those of us who are capable of producing, can produce and provide to them! Therefore, producing or prospering, becomes a moral obligation for those of us who can do so (even if we do not want or need any more for ourselves), for without our prosperity and charity these people would surely perish.

On the other hand, there are also people in the world who could learn these principles and be more self-sufficient, but refuse to be, because they are too spoiled, lazy, irresponsible, arrogant, hard-headed or selfish do so! With the "terminally needy," they need fish after fish! Now, I'm not saying you should ever let them go hungry, but if you keep on feeding them they will never learn how to fish on their own, which is a great injustice to them! Perhaps you should encourage them to read this book so they can learn how to fish on their own? Believe me, in the long run you will be happier and so will they!

IV

GOD'S SUPPLY IS INFINITE

God's supply is infinite, with more than enough to meet the demands each of us places upon it. In fact, when more is needed, more is simply produced or brought forth from the invisible, as in the multiplication of the fishes and the loaves. In the invisible substance of your imagination, there exists a vast and never-ending supply that can be called forth into visibility by you at any time you choose! If you can imagine it and believe it...it is possible, because *all things are possible.* In fact, if all of God's lavish abundance were to suddenly be called into our world, our world would not be able to contain it all! Therefore, in asking for what you want, you are never taking away from anyone else's supply, because the supply available to each of us is endless!

The fact is...the poor souls who lack in this world, do not lack because our Heavenly Father is holding anything back from them, they lack because they possess a lack consciousness, either because they were unfortunately born into it (like those starving in Africa) or developed one on their own. Either way, through the *proper* spiritual education it *can* permanently be overcome!

Science teaches us that for every cause in the universe there is a direct effect. Thought is the cause...reality is the effect. Plainly put, people lack simply because they constantly think about lack. "For whatsoever a man soweth, that shall he also reap." (Galatians 6:7) This scripture represents the universal Law of Cause and Effect; a law which works much like the law of gravity does, impersonally.

Here's how the law works, as God's raw creative power constantly flows from inside the core of your soul to the outside of your being it is being imprinted with every thought and belief impression it finds in the layers of both your subconscious (where your old belief patterns are stored) and your conscious (where your new thought and beliefs are formed) phases of mind. Then, once this raw reality generating force has been impressed with the combination of your old and new thought and belief patterns, it goes forth into the world to create whatever circumstances are needed to validate the impressions it has been given. What this boils down to is this, all of the thoughts and beliefs you hold in your mind are actually self-fulfilling prophesies!

The true spiritual error does not lie in the money or the materiality, but in the arrogance, false pride, ingratitude and selfishness that often accompanies it.

The Law of Cause and Effect is an infallible, non-circumventable system that our Heavenly Father has created for us to live and operate under. This law dictates that we get back—exactly what we put out. "As a man thinketh in his heart so is he (or so he becomes)." (Proverbs 23:7) This law does not judge the thoughts you provide as being positive or negative. This means that there are no pre-determinations taking place regarding whether the thoughts you provide now will or will not be harmful to you when they ultimately come to pass. This law God created for us to operate under functions on a completely impersonal level, twenty-four hours a day, seven days a week…garbage in—garbage out, God's law doesn't judge or care. Think thoughts of abundance…get abundance, think lack…get lack, think you're lucky…and you will be lucky, think you're unlucky…and you will be unlucky, think health…get health, think illness…get illness, and think happiness…get happiness, this is how it works. But how do you think about abundance when you are in debt up to your ears and you can't pay your bills? Don't worry we will get to that later.

Jesus said, "I am come that they might have more life, and that they might have it more abundantly." (John 10:10) This scripture plainly states that one of the purposes of His coming was to give us more abundant "life". How did His unmistakable message for us to have more abundant life get lost in the translation?! By abundance, I am not merely referring to financial abundance! I am speaking of *all* the forms of an abundant life, which includes health, love, spiritual, energy, joy, goodness, virtue, cheerfulness, humor, fun, integrity, discipline, kindness, patience, selflessness, generosity, good will, compassion, laughter, beauty, fitness, cleanliness, purity, gratitude, honesty, faith, loyalty, bravery, harmony, happiness, success, charity, etc. The bottom line is…if you or anyone you know has been suffering from loneliness, spiritual destitution, financial lack, debt, poor health, depression, broken relationships, weight problems, job issues, grief, abuse, stress, pain, or any other problems, with unlimited abundance readily available, there is plainly no reason for you or anyone else to continue to suffer!

From this point forward, this book will be dedicated to revealing the original teachings of Jesus for you to use; teachings that are a proven road map to accessing the supernatural wellspring your Heavenly Father gave you; a wellspring that He *intended* for you to fully access and use for good purposes.

Why follow Jesus? Well, I am not suggesting that you follow Him because some overzealous religious fanatic shows up and tells you that you should. But, because clearly *no one* in history has ever exemplified a higher level of demonstration than He and because when His teachings are properly interpreted and applied they work for you exactly as He said they would. But, as previously mentioned, you don't have to take any of what this book has to say at face value. You will be able to try it for yourself and once you do…the results you will achieve will be all the proof you will need.

…you are already abundantly rich in every way.

When this new information first came to me in 1984, I don't mind telling you that I had my doubts. I thought, how could something this profound and important possibly be true about us and everyone not know about it? Surely, if this were true, the scholars, theologians and great thinkers of our times would have already known, and would be practicing it. Everyone would have known. How could something this important have possibly gotten past us? After all, we've put a man on the moon, performed heart transplants and now have the microwave oven! It just didn't make sense to me. But, then I thought, what if there is even the smallest chance that it is true and I miss it?! How dumb would I have to be to let the opportunity to access and benefit from the limitless possibilities my Creator gave to me pass me by whether I was in real trouble or not? In my mind, as you already know it would have been *inexcusable*! And now, I am forever grateful that I did not just write all this off as just too outlandish to be believed and ignore what has now blessed me and so many others in countless positive ways.

There isn't a theme park ride or personal thrill I've ever had in my life that has ever come close to matching the incredible experience of making my quantum leap in reality *"From the Poorhouse to the Penthouse"*! To this day it is the biggest thrill I have ever experienced! Better still, I now have the confidence to face anything knowing that I will ultimately prevail. No matter what happens, I know that I always have a way out and this is where the true value lies.

V

WHY THE TRUTH WAS LOST

Back during the time when Jesus walked on the earth, can you just imagine how difficult it would have been to teach the uneducated, superstitious people of those days these difficult concepts? Even for an educated person of today's standards these are not easy concepts to grasp, much less those poor souls! Is it any wonder that Jesus had to resort to using many parables and symbols to convey His message? For example, when He shared the truth of the boundless resource that resides within us, He referred to it this way, "But whosoever shall drink of the water (the supernatural wellspring within) that I shall give them (through His teachings and His spirit) shall never thirst (have their every need and desire met)." (St. John 4:14) He also said it this more direct and indisutable way, "The Kingdom of God is within you." (Luke 17:21)

The incredible truth of the vast wellspring within, of which Jesus spoke of over two thousand years ago, has been one of the best kept secrets of all time. But why, you may ask, has this critical knowledge been secret? Why have the *original* teachings of Jesus been hidden or altered from His initial intended message?

This greatest travesty of all time happened because of fear. You see back in the days when Jesus walked the earth, those professing to have any kind of power (much less the kind that could move mountains and raise the dead), were perceived to be a threat to the leaders of those times, and as a result they were targeted and killed.

Many of the earliest Christians, starting with Jesus, were subjected to horrible deaths. Killings that were performed in full public view, to deliberately instill fear in all those who might try to spread and ultimately use the awesome power Jesus revealed to us against those in authority. These brutal methods of control were effective at causing the original teachings of Jesus to be altered out of fear of persecution and execution. Although His words have remained constant, the message He originally conveyed behind His words has not.

Your life and the lives of your loved ones are all self-inflicted.

The serious alteration that was made in the original teachings of Jesus took the creative power that Jesus told us resides within us and external-ized it. This change gave the creative power only to Jesus and our Heavenly Father, which is not at all what Jesus originally told us was true, a fact that can be clearly and unmistakenly verified in the scriptures.

When God's creative power was removed from within us, it took our thoughts and beliefs out of the loop of direct responsibility that they have for all of our outcomes. This radical alteration in our Heavenly Father's basic structure of us has left us completely helpless to whatever lives that resulted from the random negative thoughts and beliefs that we have held for over the past two thousand years! And as an unfortunate consequence of this, we have thought ourselves into early deaths, accidents, pain, suffering, sickness, financial lack, etc. without ever knowing that we brought it on ourselves.

Naturally, not realizing that we really brought all of our pain and suffering upon ourselves, we looked to our loving Heavenly Father and wondered why He would ever hurt us or our loved ones. When it wasn't Him…it was us. From the beginning He lovingly bestowed upon us the free will to think whatever thoughts we wanted to, and the last time I checked He hasn't taken that free will back. This means that according to the system that our Father designed for us to operate under, your life and the lives of your loved ones have all been self-inflicted.

Since those dark times, the fear that caused the original teachings of Jesus to be altered, along with the tradition of unbroken teachings handed down through the churches since those days, have worked together to effectively rob us of the plain truth to this day.

Again, the problem does not lie in the words of Jesus. The problem lies in the correct interpretation of those words. The plain truth is that the boundless resource that resides within you, which science refers to as the quanta…the Chinese refer to as the Chi…that the Hindu's refer to as the Jiv…in the Holy Scriptures of the Bible is called the Spirit of

God. "Know ye not that *ye are the temple of God*, and that the Spirit of God dwelleth in you?" (1 Corinthians 3:16)

What an important revelation! The Holy Scriptures, in clear, concise and unmistakable words say that God is in you! Now, knowing that this is what the scriptures plainly say is true about us, it is our job to now stand up for what the Bible says and to do this in the face of long-standing erroneous traditions. This is not "New Age," because I am not a New Age follower. I am what you might call "Old Age!" I am rooted solidly in the Bible and the proper interpretation of its two-thousand year old teachings. This is what Jesus, our beloved master, originally taught and we need to boldly stand up for what He came to teach us. If not us…who? If not now…when?

I am what I would refer to as a true Christian now, but I did not come to my conclusions lightly. Finding truth has been like piecing together an enormous jig-saw puzzle, made up of many small pieces that all had to fit together perfectly in order to get a look at the bigger picture and make sense of it all.

I have always been more of what I would refer to as an independent and scientifically-minded thinker. Even as a child I was never able to blindly follow anything I was taught without questioning it first. Growing up in West Texas, I attended a small town church and although I was exposed to the strict doctrine being taught there, I did not readily accept everything being taught. Forced to go, because not going was not an option in my family, I sat on the hard wooden pews of our quaint little country church every Sunday, with my arms folded tightly and my bottom lip out, listening intently to everything being said and then quietly running everything I heard through what I like to call my "truth detection filter."

Many people blindly choose to follow a religion and all its teachings simply because they were born into it. I for one believe that we should question and make educated decisions regarding the important matter of our religion. I personally

The problem does not lie in the words of Jesus, but in their correct interpretations.

needed more proof, answers and substance than was being offered. It needed to all make sense to me! Thankfully, it was this all encompassing "need to know" that lead me on my journey to find the ultimate truth; a truth I finally discovered encoded within the scriptures themselves.

The important core truth I ultimately discovered encoded within the scriptures is that the very same omnipotent, creative power our Heavenly Father used to create the Earth and everything on it is the very same power that our Heavenly Father placed inside of you! Just as our Heavenly Father and his son Jesus were able to consciously and deliberately shape and direct this power to freely produce miracles and create what they chose to create—so can you, through your alignment with their same frequency or nature and your focused, emotionalized words, thoughts, beliefs and faith. Now, before you start thinking that this is just too outlandish to be believed, remember that it was Jesus Himself who called us His brothers and sisters and told us that all the things He could do we could do also and *even greater* things than those. We just never *knew* who we really were, *what* we had within us, *how* to fully access it, or *believed* that we could do those things and therefore we haven't been able to…*yet*.

Let me take a quick moment here though, to make a very important point, *you are not the power*, but merely a director of this awesome power. In fact, the less credit you take for the outcomes you experience in life and the more glory, credit and thanks you give to the limitless power of God within that actually does the work, the more of God's power you will release. So in simple terms, the more humble and thankful you remain the more supernatural power will flow through you.

"I am the vine and ye are the branches: he that abideth in me, and I in him (align with his perfect nature), the same bringeth forth much fruit: for without me ye can do nothing." (St. John 15:5) As explained by this scripture, when you align yourself with God's perfect nature or calibrate your frequency to His perfect frequency you will have limitless access to the raw, creative power within you to shape in any positive way you choose to achieve immediate supernatural results just as Jesus did. But, when you are not aligned with His perfect nature or frequency you cut yourself off from having full access to the limitless resources available to you and lose your ability to make a quantum leap.

Aligned—unrestricted access to infinite supernatural
creative power to use in any positive, beneficial way you choose.
Not aligned—no access.

Throughout history the large majority of society has *not* been aligned. Which means that you cannot judge what is possible for you based on what you have observed in others. So don't even bother looking around to judge what is and isn't possible for you! Because they have not been aligned, they have not been exhibiting anything close to what is actually possible for us. Regardless of what we have achieved so far, a "new frontier" of possibilities beyond your wildest imaginings, does exist.

Before passing judgment as to what degree of possibilities are available to you, remain open, because the opportunity for you to experience much more through proper alignment is a reality. If you can suspend your pre-conceived ideas about life and how it works for just a moment and properly align yourself, you can make a quantum leap out of any undesirable situation you may be in, into a new incredible life of your choosing. What do you think? Do you think it's worth further investigation? Then read on!

VI

YOU WERE CREATED TO BE THE
MASTER OF YOUR CIRCUMSTANCES...
NOT A VICTIM OF THEM

Is it appropriate for us to be tapping-in and utilizing this resource in this way? Well, to answer this question let's look to the story about Peter who walked on the water, as told in the book of Matthew. When Peter saw Jesus walking on water and got out of the boat to walk on the water to meet Him, Jesus didn't say to Peter, "Who do you think you are, get back in that boat!" No, Jesus *expected* Peter to be able to do it, just as He expects you to use your belief/faith to direct and utilize the stream of limitless potential that is flowing through you to the highest degree possible. Jesus always praised those who were able to do this and He wants you to do it, too! Peter was only scolded by Jesus when he temporarily broke concentration and doubted his ability to do what Jesus could do. "O ye of little faith, wherefore didst thou doubt!?" (Matthew 14:31) This is what Jesus said to Peter when he started to sink. Now, was He upset with Peter because he was trying to do what He could do *or* because Peter doubted that he could do it?

For starters, you may not be ready to walk on water yet. Perhaps you want to start by directing the stream of infinite potential that flows through you to get a better job, attract more business, to heal yourself or a loved one, lose weight, find your true love or get out of debt.

Whatever your present needs are I will tell you this—you are *not* just supposed to sit around and suffer or stand by while your friends and loved ones continue to suffer! The Bible clearly states that you are *suppose to be using* your faith/belief to direct the stream of boundless possibilities that are flowing through you to attain whatever you need or desire in life, not only for your own good, but also for the good of others! "Therefore I say unto you, *what things so ever you desire* (no limitations as to what you can ask for there!), when ye pray, *believe* you receive them and you shall have them" (Mark 11:24) "Without *faith* it is impossible to please God." (Hebrews 11:6) With all this said, the affirmative answer to the important question about whether you should or shouldn't be directing this God-given resource with your faith/belief is probably pretty obvious to you by now. Why else would your Heavenly Father have put this infinite resource inside of you in the first place if you weren't meant to use it? Makes perfect sense, doesn't it?

You were instructed by your Creator to take charge over your world.

The fact is, by its very placement and design you're already using your God-given resource whether you want to or not, twenty-four hours a day, seven days a week. The only difference now will be, to what degree you will choose to access it and whether you will now choose to direct it consciously or if you will continue to direct it unconsciously.

Should you be wondering, according to the Bible, *consciously is how you are supposed to be directing this resource.* In fact, in the first chapter of Genesis we were clearly instructed by our Creator to do just that! "And God said to them, Be fruitful, and multiply, and replenish the earth, and *subdue* it..." (Genesis 1:28) In Webster's dictionary the definition of subdue means: to take charge over, bring under subjection, to overpower or control. You were instructed by your creator to take charge of your world. You were created to be the master of your circumstances, not to be a helpless victim of them. But, how do you take control of your circumstances or your world? You take control of your life and your circumstances by taking charge of every thought and belief you allow to occupy your mind at all times. And by only allowing those thoughts and beliefs which are positive to occupy your mind, you assure yourself of only positive outcomes! Besides, all the negative thoughts and beliefs you allow yourself to harbor in your mind are actually the source of all your sin.

Sin is not just the physical act itself. "But I say to you, that whosoever looketh on a woman to lust after her (Playboy, topless bars, etc.) hath committed adultery with her already... (Matthew 5:28) Sin begins with the sinful thought that *precedes* the physical act. The origin of sin is actually every single negative, harmful or wrong thought you hold toward yourself, others or God.

You know, not taking charge of your thoughts and beliefs, is like being behind the steering wheel of your car that is speeding down the road and then refusing to put your hands on the wheel. Now, what person in their right mind would do that in their car? Yet we do it everyday with our lives?! If you were doing things the way your Father wanted you to, you wouldn't just sit there with your wheels spinning going nowhere, or worse yet, allowing your life to careen out of control as if you have nothing to do with it! No, if you were doing things correctly, you would be taking charge of your thoughts, driving your life in a positive direction as your Father wants you to do!

When we refuse to drive and end up in a big heap, we use sayings such as, "It all must have been part of God's plan" or "God must have had a reason" to comfort ourselves. Well, I can tell you it was never part of God's plan for us to let go of the steering wheel and end up in a giant mess, sick, financially destitute, depressed, hurt, overwhelmed, miserable or dead in the first place! No. We did that because of our own ignorance! But we don't have to do that anymore. Anyone who wants to—can learn how to take charge of their thoughts and drive safely to the positive destination of their choosing. Just do what your Father wanted you to do in the first place, and that is to choose good destinations for your life and then drive yourself safely to them by holding only good thoughts and positive beliefs regarding your desired outcomes.

The really good news in all of this is that…if you thought yourself into your mess, then you can certainly think yourself right out of it! Now that is a good piece of news isn't it?!

All this said and even though it makes no sense at all, there will still be those who won't get a grip, heed what they have read, and take charge of their thoughts and beliefs! Even though you would have to be dumb as a grape not to do so at this point, knowing what you know now!

☙

Garbage-in,
Garbage-out,
the system doesn't care!

Hey, I'm not saying this to be mean. I'm saying this because I happen to know first hand what sort of tragedy can result from random, reckless negative thinking and I don't want what happened to me, to happen to anyone else!

In 1984 I had successfully thought myself right into cancer, obesity, financial destitution, depression, no job, no car, an eviction, and no where to turn! "The thing which I greatly feared is come upon me." (Job 3:25)

How can I be absolutely sure that my thoughts were connected to these unfortunate outcomes? Because, by carefully tracing back my thoughts that preceded my negative circumstances, I could clearly see the connection to the negative thoughts I'd consistently held about my weight, my health, my finances, job, car, and living situation and what had happened in my life! They were a perfect match. Garbage-in, garbage-out. The system God created for us to operate under didn't care. It had just taken what I fed to it and produced the correlating outcome, plain and simple. As much as I didn't want to face the fact that I had thought myself into my mess, I had to, in order to believe that I could think myself out of it! Which of course is what I did.

VII

A NEW LIFEPRINT EQUALS
A NEW LIFE

Your current field of individualized consciousness is like a "lifeprint" of you. A unique, personal imprint of your current belief system; how healthy you are, shy, outgoing, successful, lucky, unlucky, smart, athletic, loved, happy, prosperous, including the new goals you have for yourself. As God's raw, creative power flows through you, it reads all your old and new thought and belief impressions and then goes forth and validates them for you in your future. This is what it does. This is its job—a job it does relentlessly, ceaselessly and impersonally. So you see that you cannot stop the process from happening simply because you have decided that you do not want to participate. In fact, you are participating at this very moment!

What this all boils down to is this, every single thought and belief you hold to be true about yourself, your life and your future, are actually directives—self-provided directives that are being continually read and validated for you in your future by the most powerful, intricate, creative process in existence! This means that, not only are you in charge of your life right now…you have always been in charge of your life (albeit unknowingly in most cases). You are now, and always have been, the creator of the lifeprint for your life! Want a new life? Hey, no problem, just create a new lifeprint for yourself. New lifeprint—new life! Or, don't change your lifeprint at all and keep on getting more of what you have been getting, it's your choice.

You're in charge whether you want to be or not.

The scriptures put it this way, "Be ye transformed by the renewing of your mind." (Romans 12:2) One of the most radical examples of this scripture would be the unusual condition known as Multiple

Personality Complex. With this rare condition the individual has several different "lifeprints" or separate identities that basically take turns living in the same body.

Each lifeprint or identity is separate and unique, each one possessing a completely different set of personality and physical characteristics. As each of the different identities take turns inhabiting the same body radical changes can be observed both in the personality and physical characteristics. Some of the personalities, for example, may be shy while others are very outgoing. But even more shocking than this are the physical changes that take place.

As the person shifts from one personality to the next there are radical changes in the body that have been medically documented to happen instantaneously. For example in one personality, a breast lump may form that dematerializes when another personality takes over. When given allergy tests, some of the personalities may have allergies that none of the other personalities have.

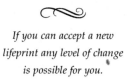

If you can accept a new lifeprint any level of change is possible for you.

Some of the personalities have been tested to be nearsighted while others are farsighted. Now, it is the same body--but what happens to the body when the mind changes? Where the mind goes, the body and life will soon follow. That is the law. A law that works every time, for everyone who puts it to the test.

By accepting a new lifeprint for yourself, you are in essence, taking on a new identity for yourself. Only in your case, unlike the poor souls afflicted with this rare condition, it will be purely by your choice. You will be in total control of all the choices you will make at all times. This rare complex merely gives you a window into what dramatic levels of changes are actually possible for you if you can accept a new lifeprint for yourself.

New lifeprint—new life! Whatever new beliefs you decide to accept as being presently true about yourself, regardless of your present reality, will eventually come true. "Therefore I say unto you, what things so ever you desire, when ye pray, believe ye receive them (walk around imagining that you already possess the new life your desire) and ye shall have them." (Mark 11:24) Simply put, what you first believe and accept on the inside, or in the invisible realm of your imagination, will eventually come true on the outside, or in the visible world. So it's simple really, just accept your new desired life before it happens and reality will have to catch up! It has to because of the immutable Law of Cause and Effect. This is the true essence of faith; *the substance of things hoped for, the evidence of things not seen.*

Once you have designed a new, exciting lifeprint for yourself (which you will be doing later in the book), the time-frame from which your new lifeprint is selected, to the time it will be projected into reality, will depend purely upon your level of alignment, your level of discipline with the seven steps, and your personal belief parameters. The more you can relax and align yourself with the divine nature of Christ, and believe in the impossible, the faster the projection process will work for you and the faster you will have your new life. A fact I have observed to be true first hand, in the thousands who have already done so. With the instantaneous realization of your goals being possible if you are in alignment, perfect alignment can be a worthwhile goal to attain if you or anyone you know needs a miracle in their life right now.

While you are in the right state of consciousness, there will be no limits to what is possible for you. This is exciting isn't it!? You will be able to literally hold any new lifeprint in the field of this higher consciousness that you would like to draw into your life whether it be, immediate abundant financial supply, a lean healthy body, a miraculous healing, answers to any questions, the perfect solution to a business or personal dilemma, your true love, your perfect work, a goal to triple your business, the perfect new home with all of the specific amenities you would like to have, and a beautiful, safe, clean world for you and your family. And while you are holding these things in your mind, heaven and earth will move to immediately lay out whatever circumstances are necessary to bring your desires forth easily and effortlessly, in uncommonly short hours.

Everything will, for lack of better terms, just show up! Absolutely anything you can think of will be possible for you to attain. You can specify any positive worthwhile goal you would like to attain, down to the last specific detail and it will show up! It has to—because it's the law. Regardless of whether your goals are large ones or small ones, there is no difference in the degree of difficulty to the resource within. So, why not go for your highest dreams.

STEVE'S STORY—A TRUE STORY
OF MIRACULOUS HEALING

I met Steve for the first time when he walked into my office, late February in 1991. He had been referred to me by a friend of his. Steve didn't go through the normal channels because there wasn't time for that, Steve was dying. He had just been diagnosed with terminal liver cancer and was already showing signs of his cancer metastasizing into malignant lymphoma. He was given only weeks to live. His appearance startled me; he was a strange, pale yellow color, had dark sunken eyes and could barely walk and talk he was so weak.

I gave Steve the complete seminar that I usually reserved for large auditoriums full of people. At the end of my presentation, Steve seemed to be willing to apply what he had learned. I worked with Steve to create some special tools (which are available in the back of this book) for him to apply the principles he would need to make his miraculous quantum leap from death's door back to health.

When Steve left my office that day I did not know if I would ever see him again. Weeks went by with no report of his progress and I couldn't help but wonder if he was still alive. Six weeks later I finally received a phone call from Steve. The first words out of his mouth were, "Kay are you sitting down?" I said, "Yes, who is this?" and he said, "This is Steve, the guy that had the liver cancer and I am calling to tell you that my cancer is gone without a trace and my doctors want to talk to you!" I was overcome with joy and sobbed so hard that I could not even speak.

I was ecstatic that Steve had mastered the teachings and that with them he had been able to overcome certain death. I will never forget that joyous moment for the rest of my life! Later, I did talk with Steve's doctors. Some were open to the principles and some were not. Those who were open to these concepts were astonished to learn about the amazing correlation between science and faith, and the timeless principles of God.

Realizing the importance of getting the medical documentation of Steve's case as proof for the skeptics, I asked Steve if he would mind if I had the copies of his records and he gladly gave them to me. Included among the reams of medical records, was a copy of a letter that was addressed from E.L. Middleman, M.D. to James Collins, M.D. regarding Steve's remarkable medical circumstances. In the letter the doctor actually used the word *mystified* to describe what had happened in Steve's case and cautioned Steve that his circumstances were, in a word...*unusual*. Here is the actual photo copy of the letter regarding Steve's miraculous healing for you to read:

Diagnostic Clinic
of Houston, ps

April 15, 1991

James Collins, M.D.
5620 Greenbriar
Suite #107
Houston, Texas   77005

Dear Jim:

Thank you very much for an opportunity to see Mr. Sugulas. I know we have already talked but I wanted to reiterate his circumstance. He presented with abdominal pain at which time you discovered abnormal liver function studies and a CT scan of the abdomen was abnormal. CT guided biopsy of one of the nodules yielded cells strongly suggestive of malignant lymphoma and I agree with that based on the review of Dr. Balsaver and me.

The bone marrow aspirate showed lymphocytosis but the bone marrow biopsy was normal. Because he felt so well, a repeat SMA and a repeat CT scan of the abdomen was obtained. Each was normal.

I think at this point a judicial observation is the appropriate course. I must say I am somewhat mystified but nevertheless I will follow him for the time being. I have cautioned him that his circumstances are unusual and we do not need to watch him closely for the appearance of malignant lymphoma.

Again thank you very much for your confidence and referral.

Sincerely,

E. L. MIDDLEMAN, M.D.

ELM:tbm

VIII

❧

ALIGNMENT

The loving, peaceful, happy, healthy, prosperous life of your dreams can all be yours if you are willing to learn and apply the original teachings of Jesus. The important questions to ask yourself are how badly do you want a new life and just how soon do you want that to happen?

In the disruptive, anxious vibration range of negative thought, there is a slow paced space-time continuum that we are forced to live and operate under. The more negative your thoughts, the more disruptive your vibration and the slower the time-frame between your thoughts and their ultimate manifestations into your reality will be! This delay is actually nature's built-in safety mechanism; a way of protecting us from self-destructing. Because enough time lapses between the negative, destructive thoughts you may be holding and their actual manifestations into reality, there is time for your thoughts to potentially shift from negative to positive, thereby side-tracking the bad outcome. This long delay between our negative thoughts and their eventual expression into reality also explains why the direct correlation between thoughts and reality may not be readily apparent to the casual observer.

However, as your vibration becomes more relaxed, trusting, harmonious, loving and positive, the space-time continuum becomes shorter and shorter and the direct correlation between thought and reality becomes much more obvious. Until you actually reach the optimum level of vibration possible where you enter into the pure spiritual dimension, where the space-time

❧

*If you think you can't...
you will always be proven
to be right. However, if you
start thinking that you can
even though the situation
seems hopeless...a way
will always appear.*

continuum no longer exists and everything occurs in the now. Ultimately, if you can calibrate your vibration or consciousness to the perfect frequency, you can radically accelerate the manifestation of your desires and do exactly what Jesus was able to do.

If the desire to attain your new goals is strong enough, you will probably be willing to do whatever it takes to align your vibration to the perfect, relaxed, loving, trusting, harmonious frequency. If your level of desire is not strong enough, then you probably won't. In short, your level of effort will directly correlate to your level of desire.

The sad fact is that…some people don't believe that they can change or that there is no way out of their particular situation. They have convinced themselves that their situation is hopeless. But in reality, no situation is hopeless. Nothing is impossible, absolutely nothing. Where there is a will, there is *always* a way!

You can think of alignment like tuning in a radio station. In order for the station to play without static or interference your radio dial has to be right on the mark. Being even slightly off the mark greatly affects the clarity of the signal, right? But once the perfect alignment is achieved, you have full power with a signal that is perfectly clear and strong.

At full power you will have the ability to speak that mountain of debt out of your life, to command prosperity to come forth into your life to bless you and others, to order sickness and disease to leave the infirm, to decree a windfall of success in your business and any other good thing you would like to do. "Thou shall also decree a thing, and it shall be established unto thee: and the light shall shine upon thy ways." (Job 22:28) In the Webster's dictionary, the word decree means: to order or command by someone in authority. While you are in perfect alignment, according to the scriptures, you inherit the authority to decree any good thing done for yourself and others! Do not be afraid to stand up and claim the authority that is yours by divine ordinance while you are in perfect alignment! Because when you hold back or shrink from the God-given authority that is rightfully yours to claim and exercise, you will not be of any good to yourself or others.

There are four aspects that must be simultaneously accomplished in order to achieve perfect harmonious alignment:

- Unconditional love for yourself and everyone else.
- Complete forgiveness of yourself and others.

- Flawless obedience and
- Perfect faith.

The application of all four simultaneously puts you in the perfect frequency; a frequency that I like to refer to as "the miracle zone." The miracle zone is a very special zone that elevates you above the limitations of this world into a much higher realm where supernatural possibilities exist. If you look at the actual meaning of the word supernatural, it means to operate *above* the other natural laws, which is what Jesus was able to do. The miracle zone is a higher dimension where all things become possible within a highly accelerated time-frame.

Unconditional Love

The first state of mind, unconditional love for yourself and others, is the highest of all vibrations and is crucial to gaining access to the miracle zone. In order to enter the zone you have to actively *feel* the sensation of this emotion. You have to get into the feeling of unconditional love and maintain it while experiencing the other three states at the same time. Learn to love yourself and others regardless of the shortcomings. Hold no ill will toward anyone. No one is perfect, including you, so just love and accept everyone in the world "as is" without judgment. You never know what could have happened to a person in their childhood to cause them to be the way they are, so don't be too harsh. Most people do unpleasant things out of a fear of lack, or from jealousy, because they aren't aware that theycan have it too, or out of a desire to be special, which stems from a low self esteem. So just love them in spite of their imperfections.

Forgiveness

Complete forgiveness, the second goal, is to be accomplished on all four levels. Those four levels being; forgiveness of others, asking forgiveness from those you have wronged, forgiveness of yourself, and finally seeking the forgiveness of your Heavenly Father. This exercise in complete forgiveness must be accomplished in this exact order. Any unforgiveness that remains in your consciousness will prevent you from fully entering the miracle zone. Special note: Forgetting about something is not the same as forgiving it. Also, if you are afraid that you are not able to think of everything that needs to be forgiven; then just add that you would like to forgive and be forgiven for all things you are aware of and those things you are unaware of as well. (More on this important step will also be covered later.)

Obedience

Flawless obedience is the third required aspect for alignment. Obedience is the exact opposite of procrastination and disobedience. Obedience is accomplished by consistently following that voice in your head that tells you right from wrong. The voice that is always urging you to do the right thing more commonly referred to as your conscience. Your conscience is actually God's navigation system to perfect alignment. Unfortunately, there are varying degrees of sensitivity to the conscience that exists from person to person. Some people have tuned their conscience out for so long that they no longer feel bad when they do things they know are wrong or hurtful. While others are so sensitive to their conscience, they can't let the sun go down until they make amends. Can you think of people you know who fall into each of these categories? Of course the goal in alignment is to become more sensitive. To learn how to be better led by your conscience, develop the habit of asking yourself this question throughout the day:

If I were living perfectly, what would I be doing right now?

When you get your answer from that inner voice; the one that tells you to get up an exercise now instead of hitting the snooze button, to do the right thing, to order the salad instead of the cheeseburger, to do a good job, hang up your cloths, be on time, keep your promises, make your bed, go home before having that next drink, be honest, to apologize when you're wrong, then jump up and do it right then. Perfect obedience will give you access to more than you ever dreamed possible. Whereas, procrastination and disobedience will cut you off. Scripture references: "For as many as led by the spirit of God (your conscience) they are sons of God." "And if children, then heirs; heirs of God, and joint heirs with Christ…" (Romans 8:14, 17) Heirs to, "The Kingdom of God is within you." (Luke 17:21) Through obedience, according to these scriptures, you become a rightful heir to the Kingdom of God. By obedience you become spiritual royalty and are by divine inheritance no longer bound to the everyday limitations the rest of the world lives under.

Perfect Faith

Perfect faith is the final aspect to be achieved. Perfect faith is the pure belief in attainment of the specific list of goals you have made for yourself. A level of belief that is so perfectly pure that it is completely devoid of all doubt. Not a half-hearted hope…but perfect, pure belief. This perfect state of faith must be *constantly* maintained until the outcome is accomplished. No matter how long that takes. You have to believe without a doubt that all the circumstances needed for your goals to come to fruition are laid out before you; destined to happen in the most perfect ways, order and time. Then keep on believing that, until your goals have time to come to pass. (More on this critical aspect will also be covered later.) "Whosoever shall say unto the mountain, be thou removed, and be thou cast into the sea; and shall not doubt in his heart but shall believe that those things which he sayeth shall come to pass; he shall have whatsoever he sayeth. (Mark 11:23)

Are you in alignment? Here's a quick way to test; check your body and consciousness for any stress, worry and lower emotions and if any are present you are not in perfect alignment. Stress, worry and lower emotions are indicative of the disruptive vibration range that will block your progress. The emotional state you are seeking to achieve for optimum accelerated results is one of perfect peace, love, harmony, forgiveness, and the pure belief in the achievement of your goals.

If your manifestation rate is slow, you should rate your level of application. This will give you the ability to identify and work on the specific aspects of alignment where you are having challenges. Give yourself a rating from 1-10 on your degree of application of each of the four aspects. A rating between 7-10 will put you in the range where you will gain more and more access to the miracle zone. Lower numbers will radically slow things down and reduce the vast number of possibilities that are available to you. Slow results can be dangerous, because most find it difficult to hold on to their pure faith long enough to achieve results without giving up.

Thousands of way-showers have awakened to the truth now and have proven that the original teachings of Jesus are an effective way to breakthrough the false ceiling of limitations and achieve accelerated results. They've discovered the secret to experience miracles, not as a rare occurrence, but as a daily occurrence, just as they were originally intended to be. Here are some remarkable results produced by those on the path:

• When protection is affirmed over a crop, it is protected from a hail storm when all of the other surrounding crops were destroyed.

• A woman claims divine health for herself and is completely healed of Hepatitis C virus, an incurable virus.

• A blind woman can suddenly see after years of blindness, even though her optic nerves still tested as dead by the doctors.

• A woman about to lose her home calls forth an immediate solution and suddenly attracts an avalanche of sales, making enough to pay off her house completely.

• An IRS agent decides to wipe out a long-standing debt of $250,000 after the man affirms that he is no longer in debt.

• A woman affirms the deliverance of her son from drugs and he quits drugs cold turkey.

• An arm that was paralyzed and withered was completely restored to its normal size and strength overnight.

• A man in need of a kidney receives one from a stranger who was guided to give him one of his and it was a perfect match.

• A woman in desperate need of money finds five crisp one-hundred dollar bills hidden in the pages of a book that had been sitting on her bookshelf for years.

At the pinnacle of our spiritual journey lies the perfect alignment of our consciousness with the perfect, limitless, pure, obedient, harmonious, abundant, loving, forgiving consciousness of the God source within, that very few have achieved. The scriptures tell us to accomplish this in this way, "Be ye therefore perfect as your Father in heaven is perfect." (St Matthew 5:48) This wonderful goal of unification with the divine nature of Christ, is also in part what the Holy act of Communion is meant to represent for us, *if* we put our whole heart and mind into it. "He that eateth my flesh, and drinketh my blood, dwelleth in me and I in him." (John 6:56)

The rewards of a more abundant, happy life are only for those who are willing to pursue it.

The special Annointed Ones, who have sought after and achieved this level of perfection, have transcended the veil of limitation completely. These Annointed Ones possess the supernatural abilities to; heal, materialize form, alter time, communicate telepathically, reverse the aging process, turn water into wine, levitate, and do not experience illness or lack of any kind. Fulfilling what Jesus said would be possible for all of us in His scriptures.

For those who may have had their doubts about the credibility of the miracles reported in the Bible, the fact that others have actually already done many of the things that Jesus did, lends total credibility to the miracles Jesus performed and makes His virgin birth and subsequent supernatural resurrection a sobering possibility, does it not? Not only that, it makes the precepts behind the creation theory a real and viable possibility as well.

Most people are familiar with the biblical stories of the virgin birth of Jesus, His miracles, His resurrection and His fulfillment of the prophecies. But, most are not aware of the other supernatural occurrences that would also support the belief that Jesus was not just an ordinary man or a profit, but the true son of God. For example, there were two separate times where the voice of God Himself was actually heard from the heavens and confirmed by eye witnesses. The first time occurred immediately following the Baptism of Jesus, "And lo a voice from heaven, saying, This is my beloved son, in whom I am well pleased." (Matthew 3:17) The second time God was reported to speak was during the transfiguration of Jesus. The transfiguration of Jesus happened when he went up to a mountain to pray with three of His disciples, Peter, John and James. As Jesus prayed, His countenance changed before them and He started to glow bright white and glistering (this is what is referred to as His transfiguration). While He was in His transfigured state a cloud came down from heaven and overshadowed all those present, "And there came a voice out of the cloud, saying, This is my beloved son, hear him." (Luke 27-36) And the third supernatural event that I feel would support the fact that Jesus is truly the son of God and not an ordinary man, happened at the moment of His death on the cross. At the precise moment Jesus died, the sun was darkened and there was a great and mighty earthquake. When the Roman centurion present saw what happened when Jesus died, he was very frightened and said, "Truly this was the son of God!" (Matthew 27:51-54) Throughout history there has been a great deal of documentation that would support the existence of both the supernatural realm and the spiritual realms, not only in the bible but in many other historical writings as well. But, no matter how much evidence exists to support these things, it doesn't matter because these extraordinary happenings are only going to be believed by those who can believe in their possibility.

The possibilities for your future are as limitless as you are ready for them to be, if you are willing to follow the teachings of Jesus. The fact that you have attracted this book and have read it this far has not happened by accident…because there are no accidents. It could mean that the time has come for you to become more than you ever dreamed possible.

The short story ahead in the next chapters is about my own spiritual coming of age. It is about taking responsibility for my life and my first conscious attempt to acquire a more abundant life.

I give all thanks and glory to my Heavenly Father and the natural laws that are of His creation. I hope my story will bless, enlighten, and inspire you to get out of your box and use His principles to take your life to a new level of living that is beyond your wildest dreams.

IX

 ∽

BITING OFF MORE THAN I COULD
CHEW

It was early one spring morning back in 1984 in Houston, Texas. I was twenty-six years old at the time and I lived in a relatively nice but compact one-bedroom apartment which I shared with my mother. She got the bedroom and I slept on the sofa. I was sleeping soundly that beautiful spring morning, unaware that as bad as things already were in my life, they were about to get a lot worse. I was about to experience the worst day of my life!

Six months prior to this spring morning, I'd gotten the news that my parents were divorcing. Mother's need for 24-hour care was going to present some challenges. She'd been ill for seven years with what numerous specialists had diagnosed as permanent and untreatable brain damage due to an arterial blockage in her neck.

Her behavior was unusual and difficult to deal with, one minute she would be fine as if nothing were wrong with her and then with no warning she'd become confused and act erratically with what seemed to be superhuman energy. These frequent, confused periods could last anywhere from two minutes to several days. During these periods she could become psychotic and imagine things that frightened her so terribly that it would send her into a complete panic. After these episodes subsided, she would return to normal and would have no memory of what had happened. We had taken her to numerous specialists to try and find help, but the doctors all agreed that there was nothing that could be done for her.

When my parents first separated, I wasn't able to take Mother in right away, so initially she moved in with her parents. I was still in the process of getting re-settled after my own divorce from a seriously abusive alcoholic. I had just liquidated everything I owned, including my business and home, and moved to Houston for a fresh start.

It wasn't long before it became apparent that Mother's living situation with her parents was not going to work. Not only was she a handful for my grandparents, she was also unhappy there.

I didn't know how unhappy she was, however, until early one morning. It was about five o'clock and I suddenly awoke for no apparent reason. Realizing how early it was, I struggled to fall back to sleep. Just as I was beginning to drift back off to sleep, I heard my mother call my name, just as plain as day as if she were actually in the room with me, even though she was actually over five hundred miles away at the time! The tone in her voice was a desperate and unmistakable call for help.

I had never experienced anything like this in my life and it just about scared me to death! I sat straight up in bed, barely able to breathe, shocked by what had just happened. As surreal as the experience was to me, there was really no question in my mind that I had just experienced mental telepathy with my mother and that she was in real trouble.

I rushed to the phone to call her and before my hand touched it, it rang! I answered, bypassing the usual hello and exclaimed, "Mother, what's wrong?" She said, "I'd rather be dead than live like this!" By her tone, I knew she meant exactly what she had said. With no hesitation, I said, "Get on the next airplane. You're moving in with me." With this bizarre occurrence, I knew that my mother was in real trouble and I was willing to sacrifice anything and everything to help her.

Caring for Mother meant that I would not be able to work. With no income, I assumed that my 'fresh start money' would sustain us long enough for me to figure out a viable long-term plan. Unfortunately, over the next six months, with no medical insurance for Mother or myself, the medical bills along with other unexpected expenses quickly evaporated my savings before I had time to develop a plan.

This six-month period was a very difficult time for me and for my mother. A few of my mother's more serious spells required frantic trips to the emergency room. During another of her "spells" she slipped past me and took a cab from Houston to Lubbock, Texas. Not only was I desperate with worry, the cab ride was $3,500, not to mention the airfare to go get her and bring her home.

Through this six month ordeal, I lost virtually everything, neglected myself, gained weight, became seriously depressed, physically ill, and had no solution to our dilemmas. I was beginning to realize that I had gotten in over my head.

X

THE WORST DAY OF MY LIFE

On that fateful spring morning in 1984, I awoke completely oblivious to the fact I was about to experience the worst day of my life. When I first opened my eyes, I noticed a shadow on the back of my french patio doors. Wondering what it could be, I got up, opened the door and looked out. In big bold letters at the top of the page taped to my door it read: EVICTION NOTICE.

I stood there stunned as the color drained from my face.

As if that blow wasn't enough for one day, only two hours later that same morning, the phone rang with a call from my doctor's office. The nurse said in a very somber tone, "Kay, we have the results from the biopsy taken from the tumor the doctor found during your gynecological exam. I'm sorry, but I'm not allowed to give them to you over the phone." She then suggested that I come in as soon as possible. I knew by her tone that the news was not going to be good.

I felt myself go numb as fear began to paralyze me. I hung up the phone and sat there with tears streaming down my face. Now, when I needed the warm comfort of my mother most, I wasn't able to turn to her because stress only made her condition worse. Wiping away the tears, I pulled myself together and headed for the shower.

As I combed out my wet hair, I noticed the four inches of dark roots that needed the color I hadn't been able to afford, just another reminder of the deterioration of my life. Then, as if I weren't already depressed enough, as I was trying to find something suitable to wear to the doctor's office I discovered that the same outfit I had worn only two weeks before no longer fit!

This is not the before and after I had in mind.

Before   After

Over the previous six months I had ballooned from a svelte size 6 to a size 16 weighing in at almost 200 pounds! As a last resort, I threw on a large tee shirt with leggings and hurried past Mother under the pretense of going to the store. I was afraid to leave her by herself, but at the time I had no other choice.

I arrived at the doctor's office, signed myself in, and the nurse escorted me back to the doctor's private office. The doctor came in, sat down behind his desk, folded his hands and said, "Well, it's not the news I had hoped for..."

The room went grey and I felt as if I were going to pass out as the doctor gave me my diagnosis of cancer. He said, "Our initial course of action will be to remove what I can of the tumor, freeze the area and when that heals, we will try another biopsy."

On the way home, it started to rain, so I turned on the windshield wipers and watched the strips of rubber flop about, rendering them practically useless. That, along with an engine that sounded more like a tired washing machine, left me wondering how much longer my car was going to hold out. Then, as I entered the freeway in rush hour traffic, my car engine blew up! I lost my power steering and brakes and had to use all my strength to pull the car over to the shoulder and force it to a stop. When it came to a stop, I got out and stood beside the car in the drenching rain, watching the black smoke billow out from under the hood.

That was it... I COULDN'T TAKE ANYMORE! I looked up to the heavens sobbing with the rain pelting my face and screamed, "GOD, PLEASE TELL ME WHY THIS IS HAPPENING TO ME?!!! WHAT DID I DO? WHY AM I BEING PUNISHED?"

Little did I know that the surprising answer to those questions would come later that same day! Answers that would unveil the secrets of why life turns out the way it does for us all.

Realizing I had no money for a cab, I called a neighbor from a nearby payphone, who was thankfully able to give me a ride. When we got there, I rushed to my apartment to find Mother home, safe and in a coherent state, thank goodness!

I changed into some dry clothes and noticed that the sun had come out, so I decided to go outside and sit by the pool.

XI

WHEN THE STUDENT IS READY
THE TEACHER WILL APPEAR

I had hoped to have the pool all to myself. It was mid-afternoon, on a workday, after a hard rain…who else would be out? But when I opened my door, an odd-looking girl was sitting by the pool. Dressed in white, seated in the lotus position, she faced the crystal blue water with her back to me.

She was a picture of quiet, composed serenity. Strangely, I was drawn to sit by her. I put down my folded beach towel, stepped into the water and sat down. She cracked her eyes and looked my way, but only for a moment and then seemed to re-attain a resolve that said DO NOT DISTURB!

Several uncomfortable minutes of silence went by before she finally opened her eyes. I saw my opening to engage in conversation, so I asked her if she was doing some form of yoga or meditation and she said in a very arrogant tone, "Both, actually." I asked her, what it did for her, and she said, "It helps me attain a calm, peaceful state of mind." I said, "Boy, I sure could use some of that about now. My life is a total disaster!"

I told her about taking a leave of absence from work to care for my mother six months before; how we had gone through my entire savings; how I had gained weight of grotesque proportions; and how I had become more and more depressed. I finished my story with my diagnosis of cancer that very day, with no health insurance, the car blowing up, and the eviction notice.

She said, "You're right, your life is a disaster!" and then she said, "When one is in a hole, one should stop digging." I looked at her like a dog hearing a strange noise and asked her what she meant by that.

She said flatly and with absolute resolution, "You create your own reality and you are one-hundred percent responsible for where you are right now and for everything that has happened in your life." I took instant offense to this comment and snapped back that I could assure her that I had fallen into this mess through no fault of my own! She looked at me sternly and said, "It's time for your awakening." I thought, how dare she and assured her that my awakening had happened when I was baptized in the Baptist church, that I had studied the Bible and had everything I needed!

She said, "Let me ask you a question. Do you believe that the Lord works in mysterious ways?" I said, "Yes, I do!" Then she replied, "Well, how do you know He didn't send me? How do you know that He doesn't have something to share with you through me? I have some books written by great thinkers and biblical scholars that I think will help you understand." I thought to myself, what if God did send her? What if He did have something to share with me through her and I turned it away?

She asked me to go with her to her apartment and I decided I would. On the way she told me the story of the miraculous healing she had experienced when someone had given her these same books. She said that many people could read these books, but only those who are truly ready can unravel and apply the secrets contained within them and then she quoted the scripture, "To him that hath ears let them hear." (Mark 7:16) With that, she carefully combed her shelves and compiled the books I was to read. She handed me the stack she had selected and said, "Good luck to you, Kay." I cradled the books in my arms and hurried home. Little did I know at the time how dramatically these books were about to change my life.

XII

DISCOVERING THE MOTHER LODE

I picked up the first book and opened it to a random passage. The passage I read regarding thoughts direct effect on reality was so profound it was hard for me to fathom. My interest was peaked and I continued reading on throughout the night, scarcely noticing the comings and goings of my mother or even the shift from night to day.

I feverishly took notes, referring back to my Bible for different scriptures. The excitement I felt as I uncovered what I thought might be the answers to the mysterious puzzles and questions of life, was exhilarating. I felt like a gold prospector discovering the "mother lode!"

During this time of study and revelation, my thoughts started to go through a radical positive transformation, and so did my life. When I shifted my thoughts from a dismal future of lack to one of overflowing, abundant prosperity, my rent was suddenly paid anonymously, my car was repaired by a neighbor's boyfriend at no charge, and bags of food were showing up at my doorstep! It was obvious that the shift in my thoughts from lack to prosperity was having a direct effect on my outer circumstances. I couldn't have been more grateful for the information I had been given in those books or more humbled by the charity of the

neighbors who had reached out to help. I went back to thank that strange girl, and just as mysteriously as she had appeared in my life, she was gone with no forwarding address.

These incredible results that were occurring in my life were based on one God-given natural law that is true for everyone, whether Buddhist, Baptist or Atheist. The law that pertains to our thoughts and beliefs being validated by nature; God's Law of Cause and Effect.

The simplest way for me to understand the working concept of God's law was to imagine our minds as slide-projectors. The slide-tray seated on top of the slide-projector represents the subconscious mind. The slides held within the slide-tray represent the beliefs about who we are and where we are going. The light source within the projector is God's raw, infinite creative power. The function of this infinite creative power which flows through us is to read our individual beliefs, which we determine and then to impersonally project, protect and reinforce them for us.

It performs this function by continuously orchestrating whatever future circumstances, timing, ideas, people, materials, actions, and behaviors are necessary to validate and perpetuate our old and new beliefs or "slides." It directs everything occurring in our lives and the lives of others, and is doing so every minute of every day. Whatever circumstances are needed to accomplish your thoughts, beliefs and goals are being lined out constantly like dominoes destined to fall in the perfect ways, order, and time. With each shift you have in your thoughts, beliefs and goals, your destiny shifts accordingly! Some have actually reported even feeling these shifts as they occur.

If you make some new slides for yourself and then continuously think you are on course to the manifestation of your new dreams, you will be—but, if you think even for a moment that you are off course, the very thought will throw you off course *until* you choose to think that you are back on course. Your thoughts are directing your path!

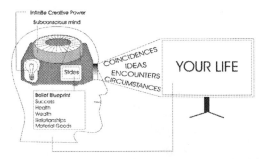

All of the negative "slides" that we have allowed ourselves to buy into such as: "I can't get ahead!," "I can't lose weight!," "I'll never get a better job!," "I'm stuck in this relationship!," "I'm always sick!," "I will never be able to afford that!," "I am such a procrastinator!," "I never have time for me!," "I am the unluckiest person!," "I just can't keep a job!," "I'm always late!," "Life is so unfair!,"

"I am so accident-prone!," "I will never have my own business!," "It will never work!," "I have the worst luck with men!," are the very reasons these things happen to us.

As previously discussed, the negative thoughts and beliefs we allow into our minds are the real cause for the failure, sabotage and misery we experience in our lives. Every time these negative affirmations are repeated they become even more deeply entrenched in your subconscious mind and thus, perpetuate themselves. The more you say them…the more true they become.

Until you change yourself on the inside, you cannot change on the outside.

Here is an example of how our entrenched beliefs effect us: Kathy starts a new diet and exercise program and she is initially successful. Then, once she starts losing weight, circumstances begin to occur that sabotage her. It could be a chocolate cake she can't resist, a sprained ankle, a change in her schedule to throw her off her new regimen, and so on. These acts of sabotage have nothing to do with her willpower! They are the direct result of the protective function of the infinite creative force.

What happens is this: God's creative force picks up the positive changes in her weight, recognizes them as inconsistent with her current internal belief that says "I can't lose weight," and then performs its duty of creating whatever circumstances are necessary to sabotage her progress.

Mission accomplished! The belief "I can't lose weight" has successfully been perpetuated, protected and reinforced for Kathy. This is a perfect example of why changes must occur from the inside out.

Nothing in this world is happening by accident, and there are no coincidences. Nothing is happening randomly or by chance. Every single event that happens in our lives is being orchestrated to occur in direct accordance with our every thought and belief, both old and new.

God's creative process is not only limited to our circumstances, but also pertains to the people we attract. We are all connected to one another and are destined to realize each other's thoughts and beliefs. This means unfortunately, that victims will naturally attract victimizers, givers tend to attract takers, and losers attract people that keep them down. Conversely, winners will naturally attract the right people they need to succeed.

When the negative experiences happen to us, they are merely the outcropping of our own negative "slides." Slides that could have been formed for any number of reasons from our past experiences. Experiences which could have occurred as far back as when you were in your mother's womb or during the trauma of your birth. You may never identify the source of your negative pattern and that is not important; the pattern must still be acknowledged and overcome. You must identify these negative beliefs and replace them with new ones or their effects will never disappear from your life.

Abuse is a prime example: If you suffer from abuse, I can truly empathize with you, because I have lived through far more than my fair share mentally and physically. Yet I will tell you that until the negative internal pattern for abuse is broken, those who leave abusive relationships will tend to get right back into similar situations, thereby perpetuating their "slide" for abuse. The negative pattern for abuse must be changed on the inside, or it will keep happening on the outside. If I had never experienced such abuse in my own life and then overcome it, I would not be able to say with certainty that it can be overcome; but I *have* overcome it and you can too.

> *Negative experiences in general are not happening for you to be punished or for you to learn a lesson...*

Negative experiences in general are not happening for you to be punished or for you to learn a lesson; they are either the result of recently held negative thoughts or older, deeply entrenched belief patterns. Getting stuck on trying to figure out what sort of "lesson" you were to supposedly learn from a negative experience, can prevent you from identifying it's true cause. Typically, the negative experience is happening because of a negative pattern or "slide" and for no other reason.

The best course of action for positive change is to identify those negative patterns and then replace them deep within the subconscious mind. New more beneficial beliefs can be embedded by speaking affirmations. An example of an effective reprogramming affirmation would be, "I used to attract people who took advantage of me, but that is no longer true for me! I now attract only people who create win-win situations." Through several intense repetitive sessions using this type of affirmation, the subconscious mind can be embedded with the new desired belief pattern. In some cases it may only take a couple hundred repetitions to successfully reprogram your negative beliefs with positive ones, however, in other cases with more deeply entrenched negative beliefs, it may literally take thousands. How do you know if your new beliefs have successfully been seeded in your subconscious mind? You will start to see new results in your life.

Once the new belief is seeded in the subconscious mind, it will begin to be projected and reinforced. Through the use of this process you can successfully make the changes you desire to make in your life, from the inside out.

XIII

THE CHRISTMAS LIST

Assessing what I had learned in the books the girl by the pool had given me, I felt that what I needed to do at this point to turn my life around, was to decide on a new exciting set of beliefs (or slides) for myself that would be in alignment with my Heavenly Fathers will.

I thought back to the scripture, "Beloved, I wish above all things that thou mayest prosper and be in health, even as thy soul prospereth." (III John 1:2) This scripture said that my Heavenly Father wanted me "above all things" to prosper and be in health (regardless of what I had been told in my religious upbringing!), with the express condition that my soul prospered as well. Simply put, as I began to prosper in my health, financially, and materially it was equally important for my soul to prosper with an abundance of love, gratitude, righteousness and charity, which of course I would gladly do.

Once I had firmly decided on my new beliefs/goals for my wonderful new life, I would then drive them deep into my subconscious mind and hold them there with rock solid unwavering faith. "But let him ask in faith, nothing wavering. For he that wavereth is like a wave of the sea driven with the wind and tossed." (James 1:6) Once I had decided on my goals, the time for questioning whether or not what I was asking for was my Heavenly Father's will for me would be over and the time for relentless faith would begin. I had to decide and be clear about it.

Fully committed faith is not a hope or a

wish. It is a firm commitment to believe that must be relentlessly held to once it is made, regardless of how long the desired outcome takes to happen, whether that be days, weeks or months! "According to your faith (belief) be it done unto you." (St. Matthew 9:29) This scripture explained that my faith is "key" to the process, which means that the belief I would have to sustain would have to be completely pure, without one single trace of doubt or I would fail. "Whosoever shall say unto this mountain, be thou removed, and be thou cast into the sea; and shall not *doubt* in his heart but shall believe that those things he sayeth shall come to pass; he shall have whatsoever he sayeth." (Mark 11:23) It was clear to me that doubt was my number one enemy. I would have to fiercely fight off all thoughts of it that tried to enter my mind or I would never win!

Upon closer observation, I realized that the actual reason for most unanswered prayer wasn't that our Father didn't want us to have what we were asking for, but because people don't really ever engage "true faith" in the first place, or they give up on their faith before the outcome has had time to come to pass! But I wouldn't let that happen to me. I would keep the faith and never doubt and never quit no matter how long it took! Never, never, never! I would pray like Jesus. And how did He pray? He prayed ceaselessly.

With my new beliefs decided upon, I would relentlessly hold the belief that they were coming forth in only the most delightful, expedient, and positive ways for me and others in accordance with Heavenly Father's divine will. Because God's Law of Cause and Effect says that my every belief must be honored, this would assure that absolutely everything that happened in the process of my attaining my goals would be for my good, the good of others and in accordance with my Heavenly Fathers will.

If nothing was impossible, what did I really want?

The only thing left to do at that point, would be to walk in perfect alignment, relax and trust God's infinite creative force to automatically handle the rest in the "best" way possible.

Armed with the idea that I could ask for anything, so long as I believed that I could remain humble, appreciative and kind, thoughtful and generous to others upon receiving the items, I sat down with pen and paper and started to make my list. If nothing was impossible, what did I really want? I put down the most critical things first, and then just for the fun of it, I threw in some other things, not really caring if they came to pass.

The first thing I put on my list was for my mother to be able to live on her own, happy and well. That would certainly be a hard test for my faith because mother had been ill for seven years and numerous specialists said her condition was irreversible and untreatable. The second thing I asked for was the complete remission of my cancer and the maintenance of excellent health, another very difficult test for my faith. Others were permanent weight loss that would be quick and effortless, to be debt-free with permanent financial abundance, and to have the ideal work where I would be the most fulfilled and the most beneficial to others.

Those first few items were the most crucial. Now on to the fun stuff: to live in a luxurious 3,000 square foot home with exquisite furnishings, weight room, a closet that looked like a boutique, a "Calgon take me away" bathtub, a fireplace and sitting area in the master bedroom, tennis courts and pool, an incredible view, security, a maid, a chauffeur-driven Rolls-Royce (I chuckled, thinking I'd be impressed if that one even pulls up next to me at a red light!), a red Mercedes convertible, first-class world travel, a luxury yacht with captain and full staff and a membership at a fabulous yacht club, a beautiful new wardrobe with accessories, and to have incredible friends and an abundance of time to spend with them.

I made this list with the same excitement I had as a child making my list for Santa. That was the really fun part. The hard part was going to be trusting the law to work as the various books had said.

How could I get from where I was to where I wanted to be? It seemed impossible!

XIV

༄

FINDING THE SEVEN STEPS

The books I had read contained many conflicting methods of application that were confusing to me and at the moment I didn't have time to make a mistake. So I decided I would first ask God's infinite creative force to show me the best and most effective way to use God's Law of Cause and Effect.

I knew that if I focused my mind on the goal of attracting the best way to use God's Law of Cause and Effect, then according to what I had learned that is *exactly* what I would get! I had already gleaned vast amounts of information and taken piles of notes from the interesting variety of books I had been given on physics, psychology, secrets of the martial arts, Chi Gong healing, self help, self-hypnosis, meditation, various religions, the Bible and even the writings of a Yogi. Surely, the answers I sought were in front of me, if I could just find them!

If I ask God's infinite creative force to show me the best way, that is exactly what I would get.

The stories of amazing feats, unusual occurrences and supernatural events fascinated me and gave me hope. Stories about people who had successfully transcended the consciousness of negativity and limitation; possessing the ability to create the happy, healthy, wealthy lives they wanted at will. If nothing was impossible, then, why wouldn't this be possible?!

With no time to delay, I made my first attempt to consciously use the law. After learning that the conscious mind was only capable of holding one thought at a time, I realized that by creating a target affirmation and repeating it over and over again, I would be able to fix my mind on the goal of attracting the best and most effective way to use the natural laws. The repetition would create an intense stream of positive thoughts that would successfully block out all other potentially negative sabotaging thoughts.

I came up with the following affirmation to use; "The best and most effective step-by-step process to use God's natural Law of Cause and Effect comes forth to me now." My next step was to focus for as long and hard as I could, by saying this affirmation repeatedly without pausing. I focused this way for quite some time until I actually started to feel what I could only describe as a connection. I did not stop at that point; I kept going until I was too exhausted to go on, which was almost two days with no sleep. Finally when I couldn't go on…I collapsed and fell fast asleep.

When I awoke, I began reading through my notes and found that I was guided with a strange new sense of clarity and understanding. The process was working! One by one seven steps started to take shape. Each one of the steps was miraculously being laid out before me in the correct order they were to be followed.

I knew with absolute certainty that I'd been given the secret recipe for success that was only divulged to the privileged few who knew the right way to ask.

I finally ended up with seven clear steps that I somehow knew without question would use God's natural laws in the best and most effective way. When the seven steps were put to the test and followed by me to the letter, everything I had asked for on my Christmas list became reality almost overnight, in ways and time that were beyond reason and coincidence.

With the rapid and effortless attainment of my goals, I knew with absolute certainty that I'd been given the secret recipe for success that was only divulged to the privileged few who knew the right way to ask.

In my heart I knew I had discovered the most powerful step-by-step process to use God's natural laws. Exactly what I had asked for!

I had sought the divine guidance of our Creator and His eternal laws and had received the formula for accelerated success.

Within only 48 hours of application of the seven steps, startling events began to occur!

XV

IT WORKS

After only two days of application of the seven steps, unusual events and circumstances began to occur in my life.

The first of these incredible occurrences had to do with tuning into a television program that was being broadcast from outside my viewing area. Due to nonpayment, my cable service had been cut off. So I armed my TV with rabbit ears and an abundance of aluminum foil and attempted to get one of Houston's local stations. The only channel I could get was Channel Five, which, I only later realized was not one of our local stations! The program running at that particular time was a medical special about brain damage.

Thinking my viewing might not be happening by chance, I listened very closely. Then to my astonishment, one of the doctors on the program began describing my mother's symptoms in such detail it seemed he was talking specifically about her. According to the program, my mother had a rare form of epilepsy that could be treated. The first miracle had happened!

Armed with this new information, we were finally able to get Mother the help she needed after seven long years of hopelessness and suffering. With the correct diagnosis and medication, she was stable and able to move in to a place of her own within only two weeks of my first mental focus!

As if the results with my mother weren't proof enough, it was about that

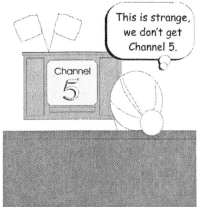

same time that I was scheduled to have my tumor removed. When I went in for the surgery to everyone's astonishment, the tumor was gone without a trace. The second miracle had happened!

This is Amazing! The weight is just melting off.

And that wasn't my only physical improvement; my excess weight was literally melting off without any effort! Then the ideal job I had described on my list appeared through unusual means. The employment ad for that job was delivered to me at 11 o'clock at night by a complete stranger, who could only share that she had been *strangely compelled* to bring it to me.

Not only was the job from the ad perfect for me, it was also a gateway to a few of the other items I had on my list. The chauffeur-driven Rolls-Royce I'd listed was owned by the company and offered to me as a perk for meeting certain sales goals. The company also acquired a yacht that was almost identical to the one I had focused on, and put me in charge of the entertainment on weekend excursions. The luxurious 3,000 square-foot town home in one of the finest neighborhoods in Houston, was offered to me for $400 a month, all bills paid, for seven years. The town home was purchased as a corporate investment and was in need of extensive renovations. I could live there at the reduced rate if I would coordinate and supervise the improvements.

The fact that the majority of the items on my list had appeared so quickly was certainly exciting but also somewhat disconcerting. My life and my reality as I had always known it were now forever altered. The previously unproven idea that thought and belief had a direct effect on reality was now a sobering fact. The rapid accomplishment of all these seemingly impossible goals meant that coincidence was simply not a possibility. It unquestionably had happened by design with the aid of a higher power; more incredible and powerful than anything I could possibly fathom.

The fact that the items from my "Christmas list" had appeared in such perfect detail was also a very strong testimony to the potency of God's Law of Cause and Effect and the effectiveness of the seven steps.

The elegant town home I moved into was located in a private, gate-guarded, upscale neighborhood. It came beautifully landscaped and fully furnished; complete with fabulous art on the walls, a fully equipped weight room, a closet that looked like a boutique, a "Calgon take me away" marble bathtub, a remote control fireplace and sitting area in the spacious master bedroom (I could lay in bed and light the fireplace!), tennis courts and pool, incredible views and security. Along with all the latest modern conveniences; push-button power drape draws, built-in intercoms, high-tech sound systems inside and out and surveillance cameras. The renovations went quickly and were barely an inconvenience.

I also had the perfect job for me. Again, specifically what I'd request-ed. I absolutely loved my work. I did work hard but it was very finan-cially rewarding, fun, and challenged me to stretch and grow.

The yacht I cruised for the company on the weekend excursions—was no dingy! It was fifty-five feet of shear, majestic luxury; with mahogany wet bar, an elegant master suite, a fully equipped kitchen and wine cellar. It was also moored at the most exclusive yacht club in the area and I socialized with the elite. It was a tough job, but somebody had to do it!

The Rolls-Royce was also an uncanny match, right down to the black exterior with tan hides I'd specifically listed, with a chauffeur named Leo. My con-vertible Mercedes was also a per-fect match, red in color with tan leather interior. I used to love driving that car with the top down with the sun shining on my face and the wind in my hair.

When I traveled, which was extensively, it was always first class with limousines and five-star hotels (the kind that have plush bathrobes, turn back your bed for you and leave the chocolates on your pillow).

All of this, while enjoying a closer relationship with God, my good health, a svelte new figure and the joy of knowing that my mother was enjoying her new found life as well (which were of course the most important things to me at the time).

The seven steps are truly remarkable. They have been proven to work just as well for everyone who had the initiative to acquire and follow them, which is well into the thousands now, and they can work for you too.

XVI

 ∽

THE DOOR TO LIMITLESS POSSIBILITIES
IS OPENED WITH THE SEVEN SECRET STEPS

The seven hidden steps to miracles have proven themselves to work for everyone who has applied them and they will work just the same for you as they have for others, because the equipment God gave to others is no different than yours!

These true stories will give you just a few varied examples of God's power at work and show you what is possible with the seven secret steps that are contained in this book.

Reading these stories will be an extremely beneficial and mind expanding experience, revealing to you glimpses of what is possible for you and others close to you who may be in need, if you are willing to get out of the box, apply the teachings and promises of Jesus and believe.

THE MIRACULOUS HEALING

Sandra Stover was in a horrific car crash at the age of twenty-nine that completely destroyed her once happy life. Up until this tragic accident she had always been the picture of physical health, active in her country club's tennis team, jogging three miles a day and working out in the gym. She worked in pharmaceutical sales and was one of the top earners in her field. She was happily married to a wonderful man and they were making plans to start their family. Life for Sandra and her husband was picture perfect.

Then, one rainy night on her way home from the grocery store, just blocks from her house, a drunk driver ran a red light and broad-sided Sandra, sending her reeling out of control into a light pole. It took the paramedics over an hour to cut Sandra out of the car.

She did manage to live and heal, but as a result of the accident she suffered with chronic neck pain that was so severe at times she wanted to die. She tried standard medicine, alternative medicines, acupuncture, hypnosis and spiritual healers, but all to no avail. Then, when she was about to lose all hope a friend told her about the seven hidden steps to miracles and she decided as a last resort to give them a try.

Sandra went through the seven steps giving each one her very best effort. When she prepared her "Christmas" list, she kept it simple and only asked for two things, to be healed and to have her life back the way it was.

She would put herself in a trance-like state of faith daily, and would focus for hours on end. She later told me that it was during one of these highly emotionalized states that a golden light filled her body with warmth and it was at that point that she knew she would be healed. Just three days later after this wonderful revelation, she slipped in the shower and seriously injured her neck, again! But, was it really an accident or God's perfect power at work?

The orthopedic surgeon on call that morning in the emergency room was one of the best. He masterfully installed an external fixator device during her surgery to support her broken neck while it healed. It was a strange device that was actually screwed into her cranium with external rods attached for support, which she would have to wear for weeks. When she came out of the anesthesia for the first time in over a year, Sandra experienced only minor discomfort compared to—the gut-wrenching pain she'd had for so long was gone! She cried and cried tears of overwhelming joy. The relief she was experiencing was wonderful, although she was afraid that it wouldn't last when the fixator was removed. But then, she decided to believe that if God got her this far He would take her all the way.

Weeks later when the fixator was removed, her husband and the rest of her family had gathered for the event. Would she still be pain free without the device or would the chronic pain return? When she came to, they all gathered round her bedside waiting to see how she felt. To everyone's tearful delight with the device removed she was still free of the debilitating pain!

Sandra and her husband were able to return to the happy lives they had before that fateful accident; a full recovery which had, no doubt, been miraculously accomplished.

SALES MORE THAN DOUBLED

Stanley worked in a sales office for a home builder selling new construction in an upscale subdivision. He worked with seven other sales agents. Sales had been excruciatingly slow during the Christmas holidays, the average sales being only one or two homes per month per salesperson. The typical daily conversation in their sales office was about how slow business was, how bad the market was, about how nobody buys during the holidays, nobody gets out in bad weather, people string you along and then back out, nobody has good credit... negative, negative, negative! They were all habitual complainers and nobody expected anything more than they were getting. Then something changed for Stanley. He attended a motivational seminar with his wife and learned of the seven secret steps.

The next day when he returned to work, he listened with new ears to what was being said. He thought to himself, no wonder business has been slow! They were all getting exactly what they were putting out... garbage in—garbage out. He decided that he was not going to "buy" into their negative conversation anymore. Instead, he would create an inner dialog that was the exact opposite of whatever they were saying and then relentlessly repeat it to himself, tuning them and all of his previously held logic out. He also followed the other secret seven steps faithfully.

The very next month Stanley's sales had set a new office record. He sold an astounding twelve homes compared to everyone else's usual one or two. With this experience Stanley learned the profound truth that there are really no limitations other than those we place upon ourselves. So we shouldn't let the limitations of others determine what is possible for us.

THE COUNTRY LIFE

Mary was a secretary in the administrative office of a large hospital. She'd been working at the hospital for many years and was only two years away from her retirement. There had been massive layoffs recently at the hospital and those who were fortunate enough to still have their jobs were working the jobs of two or more people and long hours. Mary didn't dare complain about the twelve to fourteen hour days she had to put in or she could be the next to go. With only two years to go, she would just have to stick it out.

Over the months ahead the workload and the long hours were

beginning to take a toll on Mary. She was experiencing bouts of chest pains, shortness of breath, numbness in her hands and feet and painful cramps in her legs. She was beginning to wonder if her body was going to hold out to the finish line of retirement or if she was going to end up killing herself trying to get there.

Mary somehow needed to make it to retirement. She'd never married, had no children and her parents had already passed on, so she was her only means of support. Mary was in a dire situation and could see no way out.

After attending a seminar given at the hospital where she learned of the seven secret steps to miracles, she decided to embrace the program. The only spare time Mary had to do anything extra curricular was on her bus rides to and from work. She studied the seven steps on the bus and began to make her list of the things she wanted, if nothing were impossible. Mary had never really dreamed about anything extraordinary before in her life and found it to be an enjoyable experience.

Mary searched the deep recesses of her heart and decided that if nothing was impossible, then she wanted a whole new life. She wanted to be married to a wonderful, kindhearted man and to live out her retirement with him in a small, charming country town, somewhere in the green rolling hills. She wanted a house on the hill with a screened-in porch, on a small patch of land with trees, a duck pond and a beautiful view. She wanted to bake homemade apple pies, join the church and the flower club, learn to quilt and tend a vegetable garden. This was Mary's ultimate dream. She focused relentlessly and continued to remind herself that nothing was impossible with God.

Then one day in the hospital cafeteria she spotted an older gentleman crying at his table. His wife had been in a coma for weeks and he'd never once left her side, so he had been seen around the hospital by Mary before. She went over to comfort him and learned that all hope for his wife's recovery had been lost and they had just turned off the machines. They'd been married forty years and he didn't know how he would be able to go on without her. Mary learned that day that they were neighbors. In fact, his house was on her way to the bus stop.

Mary loved to cook, so she started baking casseroles and pies and would take them by Bill's house on her way to work. Bill and Mary started seeing more and more of each other as time went by. One evening over a cup of coffee at Mary's house Bill said, "Mary there is something I want to ask you. I have a very good friend that I have fallen in love with and I'm afraid that if I ask her to marry me and she doesn't want that, I could lose her. Mary was shocked! Who could it be! She had fallen in love with Bill over these past few months and was crushed that he'd found someone else, but she told him to take the chance and if this woman was a true friend, he would not lose her either way. So, Bill looked into Mary's eyes, took her hands in his and said, "Mary will you marry me?" Mary's ecstatic response was "yes."

With their combined retirements and savings they would be able to find Mary's dream home on the hill and move to the country. Fortunately, Mary was able to take early retirement and ended up living out her wonderful dream in every detail.

THE FLORIST SHOP

The dream of owning her own florist shop was Cindy's life-long heartfelt desire. She had already done a lot of planning and preparation, she'd picked out an ideal location and marked all the floral supply catalog pages with the start-up supplies she would need to stock her store. The only thing she lacked to get going on her dream was the $175,000 start-up capital.

Cindy learned about the seven secret steps from a friend who had found her ideal husband, the home of her dreams and the perfect job using them, so she decided she would give them a shot on her dream.

Two weeks after completing and following the seven steps, Cindy and a friend of hers were out combing garage sales for different items to use in some custom, dried floral arrangements they were making for a customer. While Cindy was perusing the tables she came across an old musty stamp collection book. She had a twelve year old nephew who loved stamp collecting, and the whole book was only five dollars, so she decided she would buy it for him.

She had the stamp collection sitting out on the dining room table by the flower arrangements which were ready for the customers to pick-up. When the customers arrived, the lady's husband saw the stamp collection on the table and asked if it would be alright for him to take a look at it. Cindy was busy wrapping up the arrangements and chatting with his wife, so she said go right ahead.

Before they left he said that she had quite a collection there and asked her if she'd had ever had it appraised, that he thought it could be worth a lot of money. Cindy told him she hadn't, but that she certainly would if he really thought it could be valuable.

A couple of days later she made an appointment with a rare stamp dealer for an appraisal. The appraisal on the collection was just shy of the $175,000 she needed to start her floral business! She almost passed out from excitement.

Before she left the shop, she bought a nice commercial stamp collection to give to her nephew in place of the one she now planned to sell to start her new business. The flower shop of her dreams was opened two months later and became a thriving business. Cindy is now a firm believer in the seven steps and God's ability to make a way when there seems to be no way!

THE CINDERELLA STORY

Marilyn was an exquisite lady of remarkable beauty, charm and grace. She was of English descent and, although not of royal lineage, she'd always been fondly referred to as "Lady Ashley" by all those who knew her.

When Marilyn discovered the seven secret steps she pondered what to ask for and then thought since she'd always enjoyed the title of "Lady Ashley," now she would like the complete lifestyle to go along with it! She asked for the lifestyle of a "Titled Lady."

For her focus sessions she would light candles, prepare lovely scented bubble baths and soak in the tub while she envisioned herself dining in castles, surrounded by heads of state and those of royal lineage. She pictured herself enjoying long afternoons languishing on the sprawling lawns of fabulous estates playing croquet, and luxurious trips on private yachts.

Only a week later, Marilyn received an invitation to an elegant private dinner party. She shopped for the perfect dress, shoes and bag to complete her fabulous new outfit and had her hair done. She said on that particular night that she felt special, like Cinderella on her way to the ball!

When she arrived, the room was buzzing with chatter about one of the world's most eligible men coming that night, who happened to be a handsome Duke. When he arrived and made his grand entrance down the front steps, all of the eligible ladies were lined up like they were fighting for position to catch a wedding bouquet. Marilyn was standing on the opposite side chatting with a friend. When she turned to see what all the commotion was about, that's when she and the Duke's eyes met for the first time. In a word, it was "magical." Her heart swooned and she felt a definite connection with this man.

Later that evening after making his way through the crowd with polite introductions, he finally made his way over to Marilyn. Once their eyes met again, they were inseparable for the rest of the evening. The romance of the century had begun.

Marilyn was swept off her feet into a whirlwind lifestyle of a "titled lady" complete with castles, private estates, dinners with those of royal lineage, yachts, and trips on the QE2, the Concord and the Orient Express.

The moral to this fairy tail is that dreams come true if you believe they do.

THE PERFECT HOUSE

Shelly loved to paint and was considered to be a young, up and coming artist. She would paint by the hour and longed for the perfect home with a large art room in which to paint. The perfect art room would be a wide open room, with blond hardwood floors and lots of windows to provide natural light. She was presently doing her work at home in a small, dark apartment which she had nick-named "the dungeon." But at least it was a roof over her head and, at the time, it was all she could afford.

Yet she still desperately wanted a home of her own, but never could seem to save up enough money for a down payment. Nor did she think her credit was good enough to be approved for a mortgage. It was a nice dream to have, but realistically how could it ever happen?

She'd heard about the seven secret steps to miracles and traded a piece of her art for the seven steps. She went right to work on the steps and made quite a special "Christmas" list for herself. Not only did she want the ideal home, she wanted an international art dealer to take her on and sell her work world-wide for top dollar. And she wanted an abundance of private commissioned work and showings in Paris and other exotic foreign places. She cordoned off special time every day for her focus sessions and she called it her "dreamtime." She said that vivid images of her wonderful new success, her ideal home and art room would fill her imagination during her sessions. She loved her special dreamtime.

Well it wasn't long before more and more opportunities were coming her way. She was getting more work than she ever had before and she was loving it. She'd found her international dealer and plans were already in the works for her to go to Paris.

She was in the middle of one of her most busy days yet when her mother called and told her that she wasn't feeling well. Shelly was very close to her mother and would do absolutely anything for her. Her mother said that she had phoned her doctor and he had called a prescription in for her, but that she didn't feel well enough to get it herself. Shelly told her mother that she could use a break and would be glad to pick it up for her and bring it to her straight away.

Shelly was about to turn onto her mother's street when she could see that it was blocked-off with city work trucks. A large water main had broken and they were digging up the street. Shelly would have to take another route to her mother's house this day. She turned up the street behind her mother's street and just ahead she noticed a man hammering a sign into his front yard. The sign read, "For Sale by Owner." Shelly stopped her car, rolled down the window and asked the man if she could take a look. He said sure. She told him that she needed to drop something off to her mother on the next block and that she would be right back.

When she walked through the downstairs of the home she thought it was great, but when he took her upstairs she realized it was everything she'd been looking for. There before her was the perfect art room, exactly as she'd visualized it.

The man's wife was a ballerina and the second floor had been converted into a dance studio for her. The walls had been removed and a blond hardwood floor had been installed. On three sides of the open space were nothing but windows with one wall fully mirrored. Shelly burst into tears and told the man that it was perfect! But how would she ever be able to buy it?

Well, the man was so taken by Shelly's love of the house that he decided to owner finance it for her and waive the down payment.

When Shelly finally got settled into her wonderful new home, she thought about the fact that nothing had happened by accident to get her there. When she reflected back on the amazing alignment of events and the perfect timing it took to get her there, she was in awe of God's mysterious ways.

THE RED JEEP GRAND CHEROKEE

Alice had four beautiful children whom she loved, ranging in age from six to sixteen. With four kids and only one income, things were pretty tight at times for Alice. Tragically she was widowed four years before, her husband having been killed in a hunting accident. After the accident, Alice took on a second job. Her eldest was old enough to watch the other three children, so somehow they managed to get along. Alice made sure that there was always enough food, clean clothes and fun things for the kids to do. They played cards, board games, went for picnics, rode bikes and swam in the creek. Everyone was happy and no one really felt like they lacked for anything. Alice had seen to that.

However, Alice was beginning to have some concerns about how much longer her old Chevrolet Caprice was going to hold up. The car seats, completely worn through to the springs, were covered with Indian blankets, the rear view mirror was taped in place with duck tape and the original shiny black exterior was now a lifeless dark grey. As she tells it, "When my car was fully loaded with kids and heading down the road, it had more shakes, rattles and rolls than Elvis!" But, a new car right now on Alice's budget was out of the question.

On Alice's next birthday her office threw her a party. They had a little cake for her and had pooled their money together to give her a special gift, the seven secret steps! She said, thank you very much, but what is this? Those in the group who had followed the steps told her that it was kind of like having your own magic lamp. She was skeptical, but decided to give them a try.

With the way her car had been running lately she decided it would be wise to put a new car at the top of the list. She wanted a red Jeep Grand Cherokee. It would be large enough to haul the kids and the groceries, school backpacks and other various family items. She even went by the dealership and sat in one, just to try it on for size.

About a month later, when Alice put her old car in reverse to head to work, the transmission slipped so badly that she almost couldn't get it to go into gear. She would have to take it over to her old trusted friend Joe, who had owned the neighborhood car repair garage for over thirty years. She dropped it off the next day.

On her way out of Joe's driveway she noticed a red Jeep Grand Cherokee sitting in his parking lot with a "for sale" sign in the window. She called Joe about it when she got into her office. He told her that it was a special case and that he was selling it for what was owed on the repairs because the owners had basically abandoned the car. How much are you asking? Joe said, I will let you take it off my hands for only $2,500, which is what they owe on the repairs. What a deal! But it may as well have been $25,000. Alice didn't have the money and had no way to get it.

Two days later, Alice stopped by the repair shop with her four kids. Joe came out and told her that her transmission needed to be re-built and that the brakes and shocks also needed to be replaced. Well, the distressed look on Alice's face and the faces of her four kids must have told the tale and gotten to old Joe's heart. Because he said, I'll tell you what, Alice just take that Jeep Cherokee and we will work out a payment plan on it that you can afford. Alice's kid's started jumping up and down cheering wildly and Alice burst into tears and gave old Joe the hug of his life.

FROM ZERO TO MILLIONAIRE

Everyone has different levels of goals they set for themselves, some higher than others. When Jim realized it was just as easy for God's creative force to produce large results as it is to produce small results, he decided to set his sights high. Jim was one of those lofty thinkers who decided why shoot for the sky…when you can shoot for the stars.

In the past, Jim had owned three international companies and was a successful businessman until he contracted a rare illness during one of his overseas trips. The illness was serious; Jim was critically ill for months and came near death on more than one occasion. It was a frightening time for him and his wife, but they somehow managed to get through it.

Upon his recovery he had nothing to go back to, all three companies had gone under. Jim and his wife had nothing. His wife went back to work and Jim sank into a bottomless pit of depression.

A caring friend, who could see that Jim was feeling blue, recommended that he go to a seminar with him to hopefully cheer him up. According to Jim, the seminar did more than cheer him up, he walked away with the seven steps and the belief that if he applied them… they would work! In fact, he was so excited that he didn't fall asleep that night, thinking instead of all the limitless possibilities available to him.

Jim started on the seven steps first thing that next morning. He applied each step with a military-like precision and discipline. He focused relentlessly. With each daily focus session he could feel himself springing back to life with a renewed sense of positive excitement.

After three months of intense efforts with no results, Jim's breakthrough finally came to him in the form of a business opportunity, marketing a new herbal diet product. At the time the opportunity came his way he had no way of knowing that it was his breakthrough. But, as more time passed he began to realize that he'd found his ticket to the top!

Money started to roll-in and his wife quit her job and started working with Jim full time. Sales in their new business were accelerating at lightning speed. They opened one store, then two, then twenty-six... all within a year. Before they knew it, the monthly revenues on their stores had climbed to a whopping $300,000.

Jim and his wife were having the time of their lives. To celebrate their new success, they treated themselves to a fun spending spree. Jim drove his old van over to the BMW dealership and traded it in on a new top-of-the-line BMW, for which he was able to write a check. Meanwhile, his wife Patricia headed over to Neiman Marcus for a complete new wardrobe from the top designers; St John's, Louis Vuitton, Chanel and Christian Dior—everything from suits, hats, shoes, bags, perfume, jewelry and other fabulous accessories.

Jim, a humble man, never forgot to recognize the power of God as his source and always gave generously to others. He thanked God daily for the abundant blessings that were being bestowed upon him and his wife. He was grateful that he had persevered with his faith, even though there were no results to speak of for three months. His bountiful harvest required great perseverance of faith, but once it took hold it was quick to fruit.

THE CHRISTMAS MONEY

It was Christmas time and Brenda did not have an extra dime this particular year for her traditional Christmas tree and gifts for friends and family. Her house was bare of the Christmas spirit and she wished that Christmas would hurry up and pass by. It was a very sad time for her and she prayed for better times.

She had done the seven steps years before and had gotten great results. That was it, she decided; the answer to her prayers was to do them again! She searched frantically through old boxes for them and couldn't find them anywhere. Finally, she decided to call and ask for another copy.

She came by on a Thursday afternoon to pick up a new copy and worked on them all through the weekend. By that very next Thursday, when Brenda checked her mail, among the bills and the periodicals was a letter addressed to her with "Santa's Workshop, North Pole" on the return address. She opened it and inside were three crisp one-hundred dollar bills wrapped in foil with a hand written note that said simply: "Merry Christmas, Santa."

Where could this money have come from? Brenda had only told a handful of people about her situation and none of them could have afforded to do this. She questioned everyone and they all swore they hadn't done it.

To this day the miracle Christmas money is still a mystery for Brenda, but she will never doubt the power of God to do His part when she does hers.

SOUL MATES

Ever since Connie was old enough to date she had one disappointing relationship after another with men. In every single one of Connie's relationships there was abuse of some sort; infidelity, drug use, mental abuse, physical abuse, alcoholism, etc. In this nightmare series of bad relationships; she'd been put down, used, stolen from, cheated on, lied to, beaten and rejected.

After her last boyfriend totaled her car, stole all her money and beat her, Connie had finally had it! She announced to her friends and family that she was through with men. She shut herself in, got herself a *female* cat and vowed herself to a life of isolation.

This dark period of her life went on for five years. Then, with the encouragement of a friend, Connie finally emerged from her cocoon and attended church with her one Sunday.

Connie loved the church and started to thrive again, attending more and more of the church activities. One of the activities Connie attended was a motivational seminar, where she first learned of the seven secret steps.

After she got home that night from the seminar, she reflected back over her horrible dating career with a completely different perspective. Now, she could clearly see the direct correlation with her self-esteem and the type of men she'd attracted in her past. Connie had always suffered from low self-esteem and these men had only been attracted to her to help validate her own low opinion of herself. In reality, Connie had never really felt like she was worthy of a happy relationship. Upon realizing this, she decided to make some changes in her attitude toward herself.

With the help of the seven steps, Connie was beginning to form a better opinion of her self and before long she was feeling much stronger. She finally decided one day, that she deserved a happy marriage and would not give up until she got one. She made a list of all the wonderful attributes she wanted in her husband and started to focus hard on her dream of a happy marriage.

Two months later, Connie was in the church parking lot removing a bag of clothes for the clothing drive from the trunk of her car, when the bag broke and all the clothes fell to the ground. As Connie was picking them up, she noticed another set of hands that had reached down to help. She looked up and there was the face of a gentle man staring back at her. Her heart fluttered. Could this be the soul mate she had prayed for? As it turns out, he was. In fact, he was everything Connie had asked for on her list and more. His name was Chuck and he was a handsome, successful doctor, with a sweet nature, good morals and a sterling character. In a word, he was "perfect."

Connie and Chuck were like two peas in a pod and fell in love with each other right away. They were married at the church where they met a little over a year later. Connie was thrilled that she'd found her perfect husband, and amazed that God had arranged for it to happen in a parking lot…of all places!

Connie's most important realization through all of this was that, ultimately we are the ones who determine the kind of people we attract into our lives and the type of relationships we experience.

THE NEW WARDROBE

Marilyn followed the seven steps for a new wardrobe. She and her husband had fallen on lean times, which had now rolled into a second year. The last thing their tight family budget could afford was a shopping spree.

She and her husband had always enjoyed a certain standing in the community...the "country club set." This was a financially embarrassing time for them. They could only accept a fraction of the invitations they had in the past. But the blessing, Marilyn thought, was that she didn't have anything new to wear anyway. She had many beautiful outfits but they were all worn out.

She came by the seven steps at a seminar and followed them diligently. As part of her to-do list she cleaned out her closet to prepare a place for her new wardrobe, with the faith that it was on the way.

After she got through cleaning out her own closet she kept going and ended up with quite a bit of old stuff she wanted to discard. She decided it would be a good time to have a garage sale.

News of Marilyn's garage sale got out and neighbors from far and wide called wanting to put their old things in her sale. Marilyn struck a deal with them; she would keep half the profits for running the sale. Everyone agreed that was fair and brought their things over.

One of her neighbors had gotten down to a size six at a health resort and had then gained all of her weight back as quickly as she'd lost it... and then some. For the sale, she brought over a large rack of gorgeous size six suits she'd bought, brand new with the tags still on them. Marilyn was a perfect size six! These were expensive, elegant suits from the finest stores and she couldn't have done a better job if she had picked them out herself!

The lady decided to price her suits at fifty dollars apiece. Marilyn's plan was to buy the suits herself with the money she would make from the garage sale, paying her neighbor the agreed twenty-five dollars per suit. Voila! She had her new wardrobe and didn't even have to shop for it along with all the money needed to pay for it and then some.

Marilyn said that it was fascinating how God could organize the circumstances to make a way for us to receive the things we ask for in faith.

THE SEVEN STEPS

THE SEVEN STEP PROCESS

ORIENTATION

This spiritual system is a sequential process, comprised of seven steps. They are the same seven steps that were originally used by Kay Haugen to facilitate a quantum leap in her life. Steps that have now been used by thousands upon thousands to achieve their goals and dreams as well.

UNLOCKING THE DOOR TO INFINITE POTENTIAL

This seven step formula is a powerful and proven combination that opens the door to the immense potential within you. Each of the seven steps is a necessary tumbler that must fall into place in order to unlock the door that leads to a world of miraculous, supernatural possibilities. A wonderful new world where it is possible for anything you ask for or need to be miraculously and instantaneously provided in loving and beneficial ways that are a blessing to all concerned. This powerful combination only works, however, when applied specifically as instructed. Each of the seven steps plays a crucial role and must be performed simultaneously with all of the others. Leaving even one step out or neglecting to follow the steps in their entirety will cause faulty or lim-

> "We all have possibilities we don't know about. We can do things we don't even dream we can do."
> Dale Carnegie

ited results. This spiritual system has been tested successfully for years by literally thousands and it is this combination, and only this combination, that provides enough force to redirect God's creative stream of infinite possibility to accomplish your goals with the expediency of a quantum leap.

REDIRECTING GOD'S CREATIVE STREAM

God's creative stream already has a lifeprint to project. It is presently projecting your current subconscious lifeprint with all of its present limitations and undesired patterns and is impersonally and diligently doing so, 24-hours-a-day. To make a change, it is not an easy task to relentlessly hold your new desired lifeprint in place long enough for God's creative power to have the time to project it into reality. The precise seven step process needed for this incredible process to take place, with quantum leap potential, must be followed with great precision. If you intend to succeed, you must make the commitment to do so. Many people drift casually from one school of thought to another, attending endless seminars and reading one book after another never giving any school of thought their full attention. As a result they never enter into the all important application phase of their spiritual growth. For best results, you should commit to follow *only the Seven Steps* for the time being. The *Seven Steps* will provide you with the proven know-how and process you need to achieve any level of success.

"If thou canst believe, all things are possible to him that believeth."
Bible, Mark 9:23

YOUR LEVEL OF COMMITMENT DETERMINES YOUR RESULTS

Your commitment to this program is going to determine your results. It's all here for you, laid out perfectly step-by-step. How well these steps are followed will vary widely from person to person. Results will be directly commensurate with your efforts.

STEP ONE

⁘

REALIZE THE TRUE POTENTIAL
OF GOD'S NATURAL LAWS

Many of us at this point in history have not been introduced to the
ultimate potential of God's natural laws. The human psyche and its
relationship to those laws will probably be the true "final frontier" that
we as human kind will explore. Now more than ever, we all seem to be
more open to putting aside old superstitions and understanding God's
natural laws and the immense reservoir of potential available to us.

Unlocking and harnessing the vast possibilities available to all of us,
begins with the deeper understanding of the mechanics of the mind.
The projector is an excellent model to represent the basic functions of
the human mind. It will help you understand the natural system God
has created for us to operate under. Specifically, how the human mind
works in relationship to God's laws and reality.

THE UNLIMITED PROJECTION SOURCE
As previously revealed, God's "light" or supernatural creative power is
a limitless resource. A resource which can produce or draw into your
life whatever circumstances are needed to project any set of new goals
you provide. Reviewing the illustration of the mental projector, the
slides represent your internal, thoughts, beliefs and images. The screen
represents your life or your reality and God's creative power is represented by the projection bulb. This incredible light source has the limitless ability to effortlessly project whatever thoughts, images or goals
you choose to hold in its creative field. God's creative light is a stream
of pure, unimpressed, impersonal, supernatural creative energy that is
continually flowing from the core of your being, traveling through both
your subconscious and conscious layers of mind. As it passes through

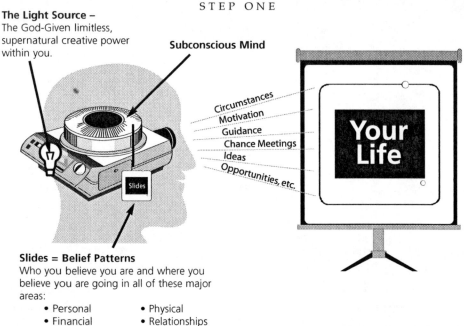

The Light Source –
The God-Given limitless, supernatural creative power within you.

Subconscious Mind

Circumstances
Motivation
Guidance
Chance Meetings
Ideas
Opportunities, etc.

Your Life

Slides

Slides = Belief Patterns
Who you believe you are and where you believe you are going in all of these major areas:

- Personal
- Financial
- Material
- Physical
- Relationships
- Career

your field of individualized consciousness, it is reading the past and present thought and belief impressions that you provide. Then, the creative force goes to work to align all of the circumstances necessary to project those thought and belief impressions into reality; putting you in the right place, at the right time and bringing about circumstances that wouldn't have otherwise happened to bring them to pass. Based on our current knowledge and understanding, God's creative power is connected to infinite resources of knowledge, wisdom, intuition, intelligence, creativity, possibility and power which cannot be seen or perceived by us with our present level of awareness. This would of course, offer a reasonable explanation as to where all of our "new ideas" originate from. Do you ever recall a time when you've heard someone say, *"The idea just popped into my head."* Where did that idea come from? Have you ever wondered that? If the solution did not exist here in a book or through other pre-existing knowledge, then it had to exist *somewhere* or it could not have been resourced. We will refer to this resource as infinite intelligence. In reality, there is not a question or problem you can have to which the answer does not exist. The all-knowing power of God, through its connection to infinite intelligence, knows all the answers and solutions to every problem and can provide the information to anyone who knows the correct way to ask.

THE INTUITIVE CONNECTION

In addition to this connection to infinite knowledge we have evidence of a vast unconscious intuitive network which connects us all. You can think of it like an enormous mental internet, because our modern day computer internet is very similar to its incredible function. Only this vast mental internet, has no wiring and is far more advanced and complex than any computer internet in existence; having the incomprehensible ability to simultaneously orchestrate every move of every person on the surface of planet earth. It is like an enormous auto-pilot system which guides us all, according to the diverse lifeprints each one of us gives to it. Causing us to come together at precise moments to either bless or harm one another according to whatever our individual lifeprints call for. There are no accidents in life and absolutely nothing is happening randomly or by coincidence. Everything that occurs in our lives is happening according to a grand design more fantastic than you can even imagine and we are all the designers. Most of the time the existence of this immense inter-connection between us all, is hidden below the surface of our awareness. However on occasion there are small glimpses of its awesome reality. For example, have you ever called someone and they said, *"I was just thinking about you"* or can you

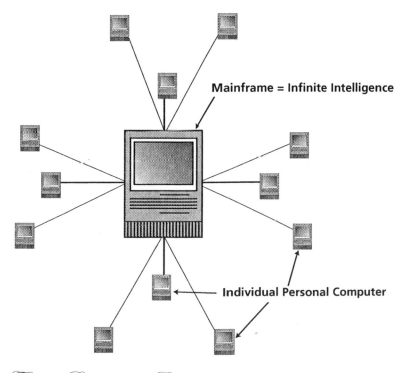

Mainframe = Infinite Intelligence

Individual Personal Computer

recall hearing someone say, *"I just got the feeling something was wrong?"* These occurrences are usually referred to as coincidence by the untrained eye. However, they are not. They are concrete evidence of a greater connection that exists between us. Because the majority of the populous is still unconscious of the fact that our thoughts and beliefs are creating the realities we experience, their thoughts and beliefs are still very undisciplined, reckless and random. Many are holding detrimental beliefs about life, such as those that say that "accidents just happen" and "you never know what the future holds." Well, if beliefs are self-fulfilling prophesies, then wouldn't this mean that for these poor souls random accidents are going to be a possibility, and won't their futures be open to all random manners of illness, trouble, tragedy and disappointments?

Because society has accepted these detrimental beliefs as being generally true for us, people have unfortunately "bought" into them! But these careless beliefs, which will leave you wide-open to catastrophes, do not have to continue to be true for you. Fact is, that at any time you choose, you can decide to take charge of your life and buy out of these negative beliefs, just as easily as you bought into them in the first place! You can buy out of any negative beliefs that you want to. And when you do they can no longer be possible for you! This is the law. As a person matures spiritually and becomes more and more aware of this spiritual truth, they will naturally begin to direct their beliefs parameters toward more positive, safe, happy and healthy ones and away from those that could potentially be harmful to them. Here is an affirmation you can use...

> *"Negative life experiences are no longer a possibility for me,*
> *I now only experience a life of overflowing goodness,*
> *beauty, love, heath and abundance!"*

The existence of an intuitive network offers a rational explanation for the perfect timing and placement of events that take place in the projection process, the chance meetings, just happening to be at the right place at the right time, and all the supposed coincidences. Every event that occurs and every move we make is no coincidence; it is being perfectly orchestrated without our awareness, by this awesome directing force. In reality we have been unconsciously cooperating to fulfill and validate each other's beliefs all along, both the good and the bad. For example, when we possess a victim mentality we naturally draw people who will victimize us into our lives to validate our negative beliefs. This means that no negative event involving other people, that ends up harming or disappointing us, can escape the realm of our personal responsibility. Nothing happens to us, everything that is orchestrated in our lives happens through us, through the lifeprints we provide. Negative beliefs about one's self and life in general will naturally attract negative circumstances, unhappy relationships at work and at home, physical abuse, mental abuse, mistreatment, the loss of promotions, unfair judgments and situations. Conversely, a positive self-esteem will draw loving relationships, happiness, good health, success and positive situations.

LIMITATION IS NOT REAL

Humanity in general has created the basic framework of belief that we have all been operating under. We all have pre-conceived ideas about what is "realistically" possible and what is not. This limited framework of generally accepted beliefs is false and can only limit us if we continue to accept it. An example of false limitations seeming real would be the adult elephant being held captive by a flimsy rope tied to a stake in the ground. Although, at its full weight and height the elephant is capable of effortlessly pulling the stake out of the ground, it will not do so because it *believes* that it cannot. This is because since the elephant was very young it has been conditioned to believe that it cannot escape. Like the elephant we have been conditioned into accepting limitations that do not really exist for us. We have been conditioned to accept limitations by the society we have grown up in, that are not real! By divine birthright we have limitless potential if we know how to access it. "Seek ye first the kingdom of God [God's limitless resource within]…and all these things [the desires of your heart] shall be added unto thee." (St. Matthew 6:33) You are a child of God and by divine inheritance the kingdom of supernatural possibility is already yours to lay claim to. God has already put it in you. But a very important part of claiming it is to first realize that limitation itself is not real.

"If thou canst believe, all things are possible to him that believeth."
Bible, Mark 9:23

MIRACLES ARE ONLY POSSIBLE IF YOU BELIEVE

What you must realize to break free of the false concept of limitation is that *absolutely anything is possible.* If you want to work this spiritual process at its highest level, you must accept the idea of limitless possibility. This is step number one. This is one of the most important steps, because failing to apply it will limit your realm of possibility and inhibit God's infinite creative power. God's creative power can only operate within the realm of your belief parameters. So if you don't believe it is possible for money to just show up, or for weight loss to be easy and effortless, or for your soul mate to just suddenly appear into your life, then those things will not be possible for you. Because your beliefs set the range of possibility that you can experience, miracles are only possible to the degree you can believe for them! The definition of a miracle is a natural occurrence that goes beyond the generally accepted realm of humanity's accepted framework. If you can open up and allow your belief system to operate outside the false limiting realm, you will breakthrough the false ceiling of limitation and free God's creative power to work at its highest level. Any goal you can possibly think of, no matter how far fetched, can become a reality through God's creative power if you can believe. God's mighty creative light has the boundless capacity to move heaven and earth to manifest the perfect path for you to achieve any goal you hold in its supernatural creative stream, so long as no doubt is present. Here are two short stories that show the results of this amazing process...

THE FERRARI STORY

There is a story I heard once that really brings home the point that anything is possible and that no goal is too specific. There was a young man who really wanted a Ferrari sports car, but had no means to purchase one at that time. All he had was the *belief* he would some day own one. He found a picture similar to the one he wanted on the cover of Road and Track magazine, with the only difference being the color. He wanted a red one and the car in the picture was bright yellow. He cut the picture out anyway and taped it to his refrigerator door. Every morning he would go into the kitchen, rub the picture and say, "One day you will be mine!" A couple of years down the road he was doing well financially and had enough set aside for a down payment on a used Ferrari if he could find the one he was looking for. He contacted the dealer and asked them to start looking for him. They called a few weeks later to tell him that they had gotten a car that they wanted to show him. When he arrived at the dealership, the salesman told him that the car was the identical make and model that he wanted, with only one small difference, the car they had found was not the red he wanted, it was bright yellow! The car they had gotten in was exactly like the car that had been featured on the cover of Road and Track magazine. In fact, it was not only like the car taped to his refrigerator, it *was* the car pictured on his refrigerator! Needless to say, he decided to purchase the car.

A MILLIONAIRE IS BORN

Another story that illustrates what is possible is the story of a self-made millionaire. When I first met Kathy, she was deeply depressed. She had lost her corporate job several weeks before and had fallen into a paralyzing state of depression over the loss. She couldn't stand the prospect of getting another corporate job, only to lose it again. She had always dreamed of starting her own business, but the start-up costs of every business she had previously checked into had been astronomical. I suggested for now, that she not try to figure out *how* anything was going to happen, but *only* to decide where she would like to end up in life if anything was possible. I handed her a sheet of paper titled "The Christmas List" and instructed her to ask herself this, "If anything is possible, what do I really want?" She took this question to heart and created an amazing and thorough list for herself. On her list, she wrote down that she would own her own business, set her own hours, have unlimited earning potential, live in a gorgeous mansion, drive the car of her choosing, have incredible health and stamina, a loving, happy marriage, travel when and where she wanted to, and to become a self-made millionaire. She went through the *Seven Step* process with precision, following every step to the letter. The first change she experienced was a miraculous improvement in her state of mind, and then within only a few weeks she came across a business opportunity that fit all of her parameters and the very best part was that it required very little start-up capital! She became an independent distributor for a multi-level marketing company. It was challenging for her, but nothing she couldn't handle. Because she had no prior experience in sales and marketing there was quite a bit for her to learn. Her company's leader-ship provided her with very little training, but with her new lifeprint firmly in place, nothing seemed to get her down or stand in her way. Others in her group became easily discouraged and dropped out, but not Kathy! She was impervious to the negativity of others, the constant rejections and the lack of training. She was unstoppable! When she didn't get what she needed, she went out and purchased several books on salesmanship from her local bookstore and began a course of self-study. Whenever she hit a roadblock, it seemed that God's creative force would always provide the necessary means, ways, tools and motivation for her to overcome the challenge. Today, she is living a wonderful life that she says is better than anything she could have dreamed of with absolutely every aspect of the new incredible lifeprint she created for herself!

INFINITE INTELLIGENCE GOES BEYOND THE RATIONAL
It is human nature for us to try to figure out how our goals are going to come to true. In 1984 when I first attempted to use the process, I kept trying to figure out how my goals were going to happen. When I couldn't figure out how they could possibly happen, my conscious mind kept invading me with doubts. My rational mind was blocking me and preventing me from sustaining the pure belief needed for me to attain my goals. I had to remind myself again and again that there was no way my limited rational mind was ever going to figure out the how or "the perfect means whereby," because God's intelligence is operating on an infinitely higher level of awareness, a level of aware-ness and possibility that goes well beyond my conscious mind's ability to conceive. My important realization about this process, was that the possibilities in the supernatural realm were not rational, meaning they could not be rationalized. By attempting to figure out by which ration-al or logical ways my goals were going to come to pass, I was blocking my miracles. In order for this to work I would have to let go and let the power of God do it's perfect work.

**The more you believe in and accept irrational possibilities,
the more you free God's supernatural power to move
heaven and earth to create the perfect path.**

To alleviate my problem of trying to figure out how my goals were going to happen, I created an affirmation to use. The affirmation I would repeat was, "My goals are becoming reality now in only the best ways for me and others and how is God's business, not mine!" I would say this whenever my mind would start to wonder about "how." My business was only to believe and I had to maintain my focus if I was going to succeed. The conscious mind can only hold one thought at a time, so by repeating this simple affirmation I was able to continually feed a stream of positive, open thoughts through my mind. This freed God's creative power to do its perfect work without any limitation or restriction from me.

RESULTS ARE THE TELL-TALE SIGN
Results are always the tell-tale sign of how well you are doing at fighting off your doubts and restricting your rational thoughts. It's not whether God's creative process works, because it's always working. It's about to what degree you work it. God's creative stream is always on, reading your every thought, limited and unlimited. God's raw creative stream is impersonal like a computer, garbage-in…garbage-out. It doesn't care. If you hold limiting thoughts and expectations, you will get limited results. Conversely, if you hold limitless thoughts and expectations, you will get amazing results that are beyond the realms of logic.

STEP ONE – THE REALIZATION
Step one is the realization and acceptance of the infinite potential of God's power in your deeper mind. Until this realization is deeply embedded in your consciousness, the old patterns of limitation you are currently living under will severely restrict the limitless realm of possibilities available to you. Step one of the *Seven Steps* will be accomplished through the use of affirmations. By frequently repeating one or more of the affirmations that are listed ahead with authority and emotion, you can successfully embed the realization that nothing is impossible into your deeper psyche. Repetition is the key to driving this vital concept deeply into your mind, because your subconscious mind will eventually accept anything you continue to reaffirm long and hard enough.

REPETITION IS THE KEY

By repeating a positive statement or affirmation again and again without ceasing, you can successfully make it past the guard that is your conscious mind. Your conscious mind monitors everything you try to tell yourself and discerns whether or not it is presently a true statement. If the statement you make does not currently fit with your beliefs it will be rejected as untrue. However, with constant repetitions, the protective defenses of the conscious mind are eventually worn down. With numerous repetitions the conscious mind begins to become more and more receptive to the affirmation being used. This is our goal. But, achieving this goal requires a huge commitment on your part. *Intense and numerous repetition sessions are the key.* The number of repetition sessions and the time-frame that will be required for a good strong impression of your new belief can vary from person to person. It can be determined by many factors such as; frequency, intensity, degree of receptivity, discipline, state of mind at time of focus, commitment level and the length and amount of time spent in the focus sessions. One or two brief focus sessions is usually not enough for you to imbed a new belief in this manner. It will probably take multiple sessions of intense, emotionalized repetitions to achieve the desired end result. Like running clear water through a milky glass, it takes a lot of water running through the glass before the water becomes clear. You typically don't wash away years of negative beliefs in a quick five minutes, although it is possible if a person is receptive enough. Until the new belief of limitless possibilities is firmly imbedded, your outcome using this spiritual process will be drastically limited. How long will it take? It takes as long as it takes. This step is crucial. You should start to take action now in the application of this step. Only when *all* of the seven steps of this spiritual process are applied to the letter, will the process work to the degree that it can for you.

List of affirmations and scriptures to choose from:

> *"If thou canst believe; **all things** are possible to him that believeth."*
> *(Mark 9:23)*

> *"Therefore I say unto you, **what things so ever you desire**, when ye pray, believe ye receive them and ye shall have them."(Mark 11:24)*

*"Whosoever shall say unto this mountain, be thou removed, and be thou cast into the sea; and shall not doubt in his heart but shall believe that those things which he sayeth shall come to pass; he shall have **whatsoever** he sayeth."(Mark 11:23)*

"Nothing is impossible!"

"I am unlimited possibility!"

"God's creative mechanism is unlimited...therefore, I am unlimited!"

"Anything is possible!"

"What I can believe, God's power can effortlessly achieve!"

"Limitation is a lie, and I no longer accept it in my life."

Select one or more of the affirmations and/or scriptures provided, or write your own. Since we are all different some will naturally feel better to you than others. Once you have made your selections, use those affirmations daily to deeply ingrain the new true belief that "anything is possible" into your psyche.

THE BENEFIT OF EMOTION
The more intensely you emotionalize your words during your focus sessions, the faster you will attain the desired result. The subconscious mind is infinitely more receptive to words that are wrapped in belief and emotion. So, by injecting emotion and belief into your affirmations you will accelerate the process.

RECOMMENDED FOCUS SESSION PLAN
Take an index card and write down your chosen affirmations. Set aside a committed time every day of five to ten minutes, using a timer or clock to make sure you give your exercise the full time you've committed to. Choose a location that will allow you to pace while you are performing your focus session in an area that is as private as possible. Now take your card out and while pacing, start repeating your affir-

mations out loud, slowly and with feeling and belief. Do this without pausing until you have fulfilled your committed time. In the beginning you will most likely feel major rejection from your conscious mind, but with patience and diligence that will soon diminish and fade into acceptance. You can start applying this step now if you like, even before you finish reading the other steps.

Miracles are only possible to those who believe!

STEP TWO

CLEAR THE WAY

God's creative power is like a perfect, pure, white light which shines through our individualized consciousness. If we provide a clear conduit for it to travel through, supernatural possibilities beyond our previously conceived ideas of possibility will become readily available to us. By aligning ourselves with pure spiritual perfection we pierce through the false veil of limitation and enter into a new supernatural realm, a realm where absolutely anything is possible.

DARKNESS IS LIKE MOLASSES
As God's perfect, raw creative light shines through you it can be either impeded or highly accelerated by the present state of your individualized consciousness. The lower emotions or "darkness" that exists within the field of your consciousness radically slows God's creative process affecting your "belief-to-reality" time frame in an extremely negative way, taking goals that could have happened instantaneously, and drawing their accomplishment out over inordinately long periods of time, even years. The darkness, produced by lower emotions and actions like stress, anxiety, unforgiveness, clutter, addictions, jealousy, infidelity, dishonesty, judgments, over drinking, irresponsibility, selfishness, fear, procrastination, anger, hatred, guilt and worry, acts like thick, sticky molasses in the gears of the creative process, radically slowing down the time it will take for your new lifeprint to come to pass.

A CLEAR CONSCIENCE MAKES
INSTANTANEOUS RESULTS POSSIBLE
The goal of Step II is to align yourself with the perfect spiritual frequency of God's perfect, raw creative light. This will serve to radically

accelerate the belief-to-reality time frame and give you access to the supernatural realm, even to the point of freeing the results you want to happen instantaneously and opening the portal for you to make a quantum leap. Jesus, our beloved Master, who was spiritually attuned to the perfect spiritual frequency of God's creative stream, was able to quiet the storm, multiply the fishes and the loaves, raise the dead and heal the sick, and He was able to do these things instantaneously. For Jesus, the time frame that existed between His intent and His results was instantaneous. Through proper alignment what Jesus did is possible for you as well, just as He said it would be. Jesus, told us to achieve alignment in this way, to "Be ye therefore perfect, even as your Father in Heaven is perfect." (Matthew 5:48) Jesus also gave us these instructions, to "Seek ye first the kingdom of God, and His righteousness [align with His perfection]; and all these things shall be added unto you [you will have the desires of your heart]." (St. Matthew 6:33) A conscience that is not "aligned" is like a log jam in the stream of God's supernatural power which severely restricts the flow. A consciousness that is not aligned restricts the process of creation, whereas, a relaxed, positive mind provides a clear conduit for instantaneous results. To put it another way, a body and mind full of lower, turbulent, negative emotions blocks the flow whereas a body and mind full of relaxed, positive emotions frees the flow. You can think of it like the difference between traveling from Miami to Los Angeles in a compact car going only 55 miles per hour versus taking the jumbo jet cruising at over 600 miles per hour, relaxing in first class, enjoying a lovely dinner and a good movie. If you had your rathers, which way would you choose to go, fast or slow?

IMMEDIATE RESULTS ARE IMPORTANT

A person new to these concepts and trying them for the first time will be looking for results to validate what they have read. If substantial results do not occur within a short period of time, they will typically lose interest in doing the steps and daily focus exercises required for results and will fall back into their old life, unwilling to try again. However, when the steps are all properly applied as they should be, unusual circumstances needed for the attainment of the goals will line up for them to occur immediately, providing the needed motivation and validation for them to get excited and stay committed to following the process.

THE ULTIMATE STATE OF ELEVATED CONSCIOUSNESS

The ultimate elevated consciousness belongs to Jesus Christ. By embodying the same consciousness of Jesus or the Holy Spirit, you immediately open the door to the supernatural realm of possibility that exists right here, right now. In this divine state of pure alignment, all the things that Jesus was able to do, you will be able to do. "He that believeth on me [those who believe and follow what Jesus taught us to do and who are willing to embody His Holy Spirit], the works that I do he shall do also; and greater works than these shall he do…" (John 14:12) The ultimate elevated consciousness of the Holy Sprit is one of pure righteousness, total forgiveness, peace, harmony, virtue, patience, obedience, unconditional love, charity, the acceptance of the shortcomings of mankind, and boundless faith.

So far, both Steps I and II can be summed up in the scripture, "Seek ye first the kingdom [Step One] and His righteousness [Step Two] and all these things shall be added unto thee." (Matthew 6:33)

DECIDE WHICH ROUTE YOU CHOOSE TO TAKE

You need to decide at this point if you want to take the long route or the short route? It is really all up to you. However, if you choose to take the fastest route then you must pay the price by being one-hundred percent willing to clean up your life, both on the inside and on the outside.

THE ULTIMATE CLEANSING

(For those who are open to the spiritual experience)

For those who are interested in acquiring the consciousness of Christ/the Holy Spirit/the perfect conduit for the supernatural power of God to flow through, according to the Bible it begins with baptism. A proper baptism according to Jesus is one of water and of spirit, "Verily, verily, I say unto thee, Except a man be born of water (a physical symbolism of you being *washed* clean of all of your past sins as promised by Jesus) and of the Spirit (your invitation to the Holy Spirit to come into your heart), he cannot enter into the Kingdom of God! (Experience all the wondrous good and access to the supernatural power that is available to us in this life and in the afterlife)." (St. John 3:5)

These Baptisms of water and of Spirit are the symbolic representation of of the purufication of your soul from all past sins (no matter how serious they may be), your invitation to the Holy Spirit of Christ to come into your heart and live there, your total commitment to good/God, and your willingness to repent or give up your sins. When you forgive others (which you will be doing just ahead) and ask for forgiveness of all your past sins (both those you are aware of and those you are not aware of) and then partake in the symbolic cleansing of the water Baptism, the moment you come out of the water your past accounting of sins are totally wiped out, erased and blotted out from the record of your life. In fact, when Jesus opens the Book of Life on Judgment Day, the accounting of your sins will be blank. The important key to the water Baptism is that you *must accept* this renewing of your soul. You must come away from your water Baptism *feeling* renewed, committed to God, and totally cleansed. Without your acceptance of your commitment, cleansing and renewal, it cannot be so.

After your water Baptism you are a clean vessel that is ready to receive the second Baptism, or the indwelling of the Holy Spirit, which is your direct and immediate doorway to the supernatural kingdom of God, through which comes limitless miracles in your life. The second Baptism is basically your willingness to invite the pure spirit of Christ into your heart and a solemn vow to live your life for good. When the Baptism of the Holy Spirit takes place (which in some cases has been known to happen before, concurrently, or after your water Baptism) there are exciting supernatural gifts, fruits and miracles that you will receive that will be your evidence that the Baptism of the Holy Spirit has truly occurred. The old saying goes, "Where there is smoke there is fire." Well, where you see fruits, supernatural gifts and miracles or "smoke" in operation in a person's life, there is evidence that the Holy Spirit is truly present and actively living in their soul. Very plainly put, where there are no fruits, supernatural gifts and miracles in operation, there is no evidence that the Holy Spirit is truly present. This is the truth no matter how religious a person may appear or profess to be, what church they may attend or how often they attend. No one who has truly been Baptized in the Holy Spirit is excluded from receiving their specialized portion of these fruits, gifts and miracles. Although, it may take a little time for your miracles, fruits and gifts/supernatural abilities to begin operating, evolving, changing and growing as you mature from the time you were Baptized, no one according to the Bible is excluded from receiving them and that would include you.

THE FRUITS AND GIFTS OF THE SPIRIT

The "Fruits of the Spirit," in Galatians 5:22-23, are those of love, joy, peace, patience, kindness, goodness, faithfulness, gentleness, and self-control. The supernatural "Gifts of the Spirit," which everyone receives one or more of with their Baptism, according to I Corinthians 12:1-31, are the gifts of Apostleship (the leaders of many churches), prophesy (the ability to see and alert a person or persons of certain future events that are to come for their protection and direction), wisdom (the ability to receive divine revelations of truth for the benefit of others and to provide divine insight to a person and guide them in the proper direction), teaching (the ability to compile complicated information and share it with others in a way that is easy for them to understand), helps (the ability to joyfully, dutifully and tirelessly perform tasks that support and bless others), knowledge (the ability to intuitively know general knowledge about a person regarding various health conditions or current life-challenges and then to provide them with divinely inspired guidance for the solutions to their problems), faith (the above average understanding of faith and the extraordinary ability to cleave to it for long periods of time when others will typically weaken and waiver), healing (the free ability to flow the supernatural healing power of God to those who will willingly receive it in faith), miracles (everyone Baptized in the Spirit can experience miracles in their own lives if they make way for them with their faith—but the "gift" of miracles specifically refers to the ability to flow the miracle working power of God into the lives of others who will receive those needed miracles in faith), discerning of spirits (the ability to sense or in some cases even see the good and evil in the hearts of people without knowing them), tongues (the ability everyone has to yield to an utterance given by the Holy Spirit for use in their personal prayer life outside of the church—however, the "gift" of tongues is when tongues are to be spoken for the benefit of the church and when spoken inside the church is to be accompanied by an interpreter so that the church can understand the message...to speak tongues in church without an interpreter only edifies oneself) and the interpretation of tongues (the ability to interpret what is being said in tongues for the benefit of one or more persons in the church). Special note: there are several other Gifts of the Spirit, administration, giving, leadership, mercy, encouragement, hospitality, intercession, service, etc. For additional information on these and other gifts, type in "Gifts of the Spirit" on the web or check the concordance in your Bible to find them.

LOOKING FOR YOUR FRUITS AND GIFTS

From the moment you partake of your Baptism of the Holy Spirit, you should be on the lookout for the expression of these fruits and for one or more of the gifts and miracles to begin to operate supernaturally through you. As a special point of interest, you do not get to pick and choose which of these gifts you will operate in the service of good. They are gifted to you by Godly assignment. Like a baseball team made up of a coach, pitcher, catcher, first baseman, shortstop, star hitter, etc., we all have our own special hidden supernatural talents that will naturally reveal themselves for our best use in, the team of all teams called "The Body of Christ."

EXERCISING YOUR FRUITS AND GIFTS

Once you have sought out all of your special talents assigned by God, do not fail to utilize them so that they can be developed and strengthened. No superstar hitter ever became a star hitter without constantly going out there and swinging the bat! So, how will you ever fully develop your special talents for the Body of Christ, if you don't first seek them and then continue to grow in them and use them for the good of all? In fact, if you love others and truly want to help your fellow man, you have a moral obligation to do this. So, no matter what anyone has to say about this matter, you should stand on the word of God, not on the words of men, and do not shrink away from finding and using your God-given fruits and gifts.

HOW TO EXPERIENCE THE BAPTISMS- YOUR TRUE KEYS TO THE SUPERNATURAL

If you have not been water Baptized and Baptized of the Holy Spirit, or don't sincerely feel that you experienced these two different Baptisms with the right purpose in mind at the time you went through them, then I strongly suggest that you find a church who believes in this scriptural doctrine of both Baptisms and go through them both. If you cannot find a church that can perform both Baptisms for you, then find a church that can at least perform the water Baptism for you and you will find that most do. Or, if you are uncomfortable locating a church, you can find a friend and a body of water deep enough for a full immersion Baptism (a bath tub, river, lake, pool, etc.) and perform it yourself. And don't worry; it is perfectly acceptable for you to do this outside of a church. There are other types of water Baptism that have proven to be effective, but the full immersion Baptism method that Jesus Himself experienced with John the Baptist is the one we recommend you use. To perform the Baptism, first make sure that the forgiveness exercises have already been performed by the person being Baptized and that they are willing to repent of their sins, then both parties should enter the pool of water to waste deep. Now the person assisting in the Baptism will recite the following words...

"With great reverence and in obedience to the teachings of Jesus Christ I now Baptize you in the name of Jesus Christ - The Father, The Son and The Holy Spirit, for the remission of all your sins." Ask them to clasp their nose and now gently immerse them by leaning them back under the water completely and then immediately helping them back to a standing position. Then the person who has been water Baptized will say, "Thank-you Lord Jesus for cleansing and purifying my soul of all sin and giving me a clean vessel to now receive the Baptism of your Holy Spirit." Then you both can begin to give thanks to Jesus for the Baptism, thank-you Lord Jesus, thank-you...thank-you...

Then, after your water Baptism, you can ask Jesus Himself to perform the Baptism of the Holy Spirit on you. John the Baptist told us that he would baptize us with water, but that one mightier than he would come afterward to Baptize us with the Holy Ghost (Mark 1:7-8). That someone is Jesus. To receive this special Baptism of the Holy Spirit, find a time and place where you will not be disturbed and in a standing position, lift up your hands and recite with total sincerity...

Lord Jesus Christ, I (full name), having forgiven others and sought the forgiveness of my Father, having fully repented of my sins, and having been purified of all my past sins with water, stand before you today as a clean vessel ready to receive your Holy Spirit into my heart.

Lord Jesus, as I now willingly and fully commit my life, to a life of only good from this moment on, I open my heart and with great reverence and joy receive the total infilling of your Holy Spirit into every part of my being, heart, mind, body and soul. Thank-you Lord Jesus for filling me with your Holy Spirit, thank-you, thank-you…thank-you… (Remain standing and thank Him while you continue to receive the full indwelling of the Holy Spirit.)

As a special point of interest regarding the unusual experience of tongues…I personally did not speak in tongues for forty-one years after receiving my Baptism of the Holy Spirit at the tender age of six. Although I've been operating freely in many of the other supernatural gifts, fruits and miracles of the Holy Spirit over the forty-one years since the time of my Baptism, which were evidence of my Baptism, until I decided to actually seek to use my private prayer language and yield myself to it by giving it utterance, I never once spoke in tongues. So, although tongues are available with the Baptism of the Holy Spirit, it is purely each individual's own choice to seek to utilize their private prayer language by yielding to it and giving it utterance, whenever they choose to do so. So, if you choose to yield yourself to it at this time, you may be able to give utterance to tongues with this Baptism. If you desire the use of this gift in your private prayer life (it is available to everyone who is Baptized in the Spirit), you can yield yourself to its operation through the utterance of a few syllables to get it started and then let it flow like a river. If you are not able to speak in tongues at this time, don't worry about it, if you desire it and will continue to give it utterance, it will eventually come to you.

These two Baptisms are not optional if one truly desires to gain full access to God's supernatural power and entrance into the kingdom of heaven. All I can say, at this point, is that there is nothing in the world that can take the place of personal experience to prove that something is real and valid to you. But one thing is for certain, you will never know the highest degree of supernatural possibilities that are available through the ultimate purification and alignment that can only occur through these two Baptisms, if you aren't willing to go through them.

MAJOR HOUSE CLEANING
This "housecleaning" process may take some people longer than oth-

ers because they have a bigger mess to deal with. For this exercise you will be making lists (on separate pieces of paper for privacy purposes) of things you will need to clean up and clear out. For this exercise you will need several sheets of paper and something to write with. Go ahead and take a moment to get them now.

BAD HABITS LIST
Take out a clean sheet of paper right now (doing the exercises as you go through the book is the best approach) and title your first list, "Bad Habits to Give Up." Under this heading list all the bad habits you need to give up, for example: gossip, drinking too much, smoking, driving too fast, always being late, procrastination, poor housekeeping, doing drugs, pornography, and infidelity. These bad habits may take time for you to overcome, but all that is required is that you start now to sincerely try. The more effort you make to walk in absolute perfection, the more access you will gain to God's supernatural power and believe me when I tell you that the effort will be worth it!

ASKING OTHERS FOR FORGIVENESS LIST
Now take out another clean sheet of paper and title it, "Asking For Forgiveness." Start listing the names of all the people you have wronged, so that you can ask for their forgiveness (may be done in writing if you like).

FORGIVING YOURSELF LIST
Next, start listing all of the things you have done in the past that you need to forgive yourself for and once you have finished forgive yourself. (Pray for help with this if you need it.)

FORGIVING OTHERS LIST
Once that has been accomplished make a list of all the people you need to forgive and forgive them. (Again, pray for help with this one if you need it.)

ASKING HEAVENLY FATHER FOR FORGIVENESS
Finally ask your Heavenly Father for forgiveness and more importantly accept His forgiveness. An important note about forgiveness, unforgiveness of any kind in your heart will block you from accessing God's

power at the supernatural level. "And when ye stand praying *forgive*, if ye ought against any: that your Father also which is in heaven may forgive your trespasses." (St. Mark 11:25) Also, be sure that you have totally forgiven all others before asking your Father for forgiveness. "But if we forgive not men their trespasses, neither will your Father forgive your trespasses." (St. Matthew 6:15)

CHARACTER FLAWS LIST
Your third list will be titled "Character Flaws." List all of your character flaws to work on giving up, such as; jealousy, greed, judgment, grudge-holding, arrogance, gluttony, lying, cheating, stealing, guilt, criticism, laziness, complaining, fear, worry, selfishness, close-mindedness, stubbornness, hot temper, lack of consideration for others, putting others down, hatred, unforgiveness, dishonesty and ingratitude.

HOUSE CLEANING PROJECTS LIST
Your final list will be about getting your house in order. List all of the things you need to do to get your house in order, such as; organizing your garage, cleaning out your closets, reorganizing your kitchen, putting your office in order etc.. Put your list in order of worst first and start working on your list, one project at a time. Work on that project until it is complete before you take on your next project and then check them off your list as they are accomplished.

ERADICATING JEALOUSY
Jealousy is the act of coveting or wanting what belongs to someone else. This is a symptom of not fully realizing that you can have it too! There is enough for everyone—God's abundance is infinite. Be happy for them and ask and believe for what you want because nothing is impossible. A side note: In relationships it is very common to confuse jealousy with insecurity for your partner's feelings for you. In this situation, ask yourself if you are you truly jealous of them or are you really insecure about their feelings for you? If it is insecurity regarding their feelings for you, then it is not jealousy! Communicating this important difference clearly to your partner can help to rectify the situation. Let them know that you are not jealous over them but that you *do* question their feelings for you. Upon hearing this if they do not successfully convince you, through their words and actions of their love and devo-

tion to you—you may want to consider moving on.

ENDING GREED

Greed drives a person to want and take more than their share and usually stems from a deep-seated fear of lack. Those who operate from a place of greed ultimately end up experiencing a negative reciprocal effect through The Law of Reciprocation. Where, as a result of their greed, they end up losing far more than they ever gained at the end of the day. More on the Law of Reciprocation will be explained later in this book. In the mean time, know that greed will only cause you to lose what you desire most and begin to eradicate it now.

GIVING UP EXCUSES

Excuses can be used by people for many different purposes. When a person doesn't want to grow up, face responsibility, be accountable, stand on their own or hold up their end of the bargain in relationships, excuses can come in real handy! Some people have made a habit of hiding behind excuses to avert being accountable and responsible for their lives. The pattern of excuse-making typically starts in childhood and is usually developed by people who are extraordinarily intelligent. A child starts making excuses for their mistakes and bad behavior, and their parents "buy into" their excuses, instead of holding them accountable to what they did or didn't do, as they should have. Then, the child says to themselves, "Hey my excuses and scapegoats are working; they are getting me off the hook!" Thus, the pattern that says that excuses and scapegoats get me off the hook is born! They have become spoiled! The phrases "I can't," and "It's not my fault" have become adequate excuses and scapegoats for them to hide behind! Now, the child grows up and is thrust out into the world away from the protective cocoon of their accommodating parents, where the excuses don't work anymore. Now what? The negative pattern is still there, but it is not working anymore. The new people (my boss, spouse, friends, co-workers etc.) are not "buying into" my excuses and scapegoats and letting me off the hook! Now, one of two things will happen at this point, one they will start to realize that they can't hide behind their excuses and scapegoats anymore and will start to grow up, or two, they will only improve their excuses and excuse-making skills to get others (including themselves) to "buy in" to their excuse game. The rebellious souls who choose the latter, have the motivation to take their excuse game to whatever level they need to, even to the extent of unconsciously manifesting illnesses (that are actually *real* by the way), disasters and debilitating injuries, if that is what they need to get others, including themselves, to "buy into" their excuses and get themselves off the hook! Whatever the situation, these well practiced excuse-makers will have ready excuses and valid reasons why they can't get ahead, move forward, help themselves or change or improve their conditions.

In the long run, the habit of excuse-making is extremely destructive and only serves to box in a person's limitless capacity for life and should be avoided no matter what. Mental concepts like, I can't, it's not my fault, I'm helpless, pity me, I'm a victim, there's nothing I can do about it, I can't change and I'm helpless, all need to be eliminated from your mental files! And remind yourself when you are tempted to make another excuse for the situation you are in, that anything is possible and that where there is a will, there is always a way!

UNCONDITIONAL LOVE AND TOTAL ACCEPTANCE OF YOURSELF AND OTHERS

Being "aligned" also requires that you be totally accepting of everyone, including yourself, shortcomings and all. Any unacceptance you may have in your heart for the shortcomings and sins of yourself and others will block you from full access to the possibilities available to you. Try looking at those around you and yourself in a new light...as perfection in the making! Try just accepting the fact that we all have our imperfections...all of us. We all have negative aspects to our lifeprints, negative aspects to which we have all become unconscious victims of to certain degrees. Your harsh judgment of yourself and others, only serves to create a negative state of mind in you. This lower state of mind, will rob you of the accelerated belief-to-reality time-frame that is available to you. Instead of condemning yourself or others for being imperfect, simply have compassion for all the shortcomings. Forgive them as well as yourself for being where you are in life right now. Love everyone including yourself unconditionally. Go forth each day treating others the way that you would want to be treated. But be sure to keep it in balance. Loving others unconditionally and treating them the way you would want to be treated, does not mean that you have to maintain a relationship with any one who abuses you, disrespects you or takes advantage of you! You can still love people who are abusive, rude, selfish and disrespectful unconditionally…just do so while keeping them at a safe distance. Remember, even as a Christian, you should be very selective in choosing those people with whom you personally connect with and associate with on a day to day basis.

ACCEPTING RESPONSIBILITY FOR YOUR LIFE

Acceptance of personal responsibility for everything that has happened and will happen in your life…is mandatory. Outside blame of any kind is strictly forbidden. It may help to realize that nothing in life happens to you, it happens through you…through your lifeprint. When bad things happen to you it is nobody else's fault. Blaming others is totally inappropriate and a bad habit that will hinder your spiritual growth. These outsiders who have offended you were only actors in your play—a play for which you wrote the script! So, why be angry or frustrated with what or who has shown up on the outside? Instead look to the source of the problem within you and eradicate it there. Remain calm and maintain your elevated consciousness by analyzing the cause or the negative "slide" that caused the unwanted experience. Then seek to change your unwanted output at its source, so that the negative experience is not repeated.

USING DENIALS TO TRANSMUTE ANGER

The use of affirmations, those specifically in the "denial" format, can help you respond very positively to the negative experiences you attract, through what is called energy transmutation. When an unpleasant experience occurs, simply recite the following statement aloud numerous times with conviction, "In the past, I used to project (the undesired situation) into my life, but that is no longer true for me. I now project (the opposite, positive desired situation)." This denial style affirmation successfully transmutes the negative energy into beneficial, empowering energy. The denial/affirmation process may need to be done many times, wrapped in feeling and emotion in order to embed the new belief pattern into the subconscious mind. Don't give up after only a few tries, it takes great perseverance to change years of negative programming. Refuse to give up and you will eventually succeed.

It may help to think of denial/affirmations in the same context as you would cleaning out a glass you have in your sink that still has some milk left in it. By pouring out the remaining milk (denying the old negative projection) before you start to run water into the glass (put in the new desired projection), dramatically cuts down on the time that is necessary for the water to start running clear (achieve reprogramming).

Typical scenario where you would use a denial...You're on the freeway and the driver in the next lane won't let you in when you desperately need to get over to take the next exit. In fact, when you put on your blinker, it was obvious that this driver sped up to close the space you were trying to move into, deliberately causing you to miss the last available exit for miles! Normally this would make even the nicest of people fuming mad. But, you can remain calm and in control by realizing that nothing happens to you by accident, it happens through you. Look at the situation you have created as merely an undesirable pattern and then repeat the following denial/affirmation with conviction, "I used to attract discourteous drivers on the highway, but that is NO LONGER TRUE FOR ME! (this transmutes the negative anger into a new positive conviction) I now only attract courteous drivers around me at all times!" Repeat the affirmation until your anger has been dispelled and your mind begins to accept the new belief. Once your new belief pattern has been successfully programmed in, you will find that you only attract courteous drivers who let you in with a smile and a wave!

OBEDIENCE

Obedience is the exact opposite of procrastination and disobedience. Obedience is accomplished by constantly following that voice in your head that tells you what you should do versus what you shouldn't do. It is that voice in your head that tells you right from wrong, that is constantly urging you to do the right thing more commonly referred to as your conscience. Your conscience is actually God's navigation system to perfect alignment. Unfortunately, there are varying degrees of sensitivity that people have to their conscience. Some people have tuned their conscience out for so long that they no longer feel bad when they do things that they know are wrong or hurtful to others.

While others are so sensitive to their conscience that if they even put one toe out of line, they really feel bad about what they have done. Can you think of people who fall into each of these categories? Of course the goal in alignment is to become infinitely more sensitive. To learn how to be better led by your conscience, develop the habit of asking yourself this question throughout the day:

If I were living perfectly, what would I be doing right now?

When you get your answer from that inner voice: the one that tells you to get up and exercise now instead of hitting the snooze button, to do the right thing, to order the salad instead of the cheeseburger, to do a good job, hang up your clothes, be on time, keep your promises, make your bed, go home before having that next drink, be honest, not to have that affair, to apologize when you are wrong, then you must be willing to follow that guidance without hesitation. By doing this consistently you will condition yourself to become much more connected and sensitized to your conscience. By becoming much more sensitized to your conscience and consistently following its guidance, you automatically gain access to supernatural power that is beyond your present level of comprehension, power you can use in any good way you choose to benefit yourself and others. Conversely, consistent acts of procrastination and disobedience will cut you off. Scripture references: "For as many are led by the spirit of God (which communicates to you through your conscience) they are sons of God." "And if children, then heirs; heirs of God, and joint heirs with Christ…" (Romans 8:14, 17) Through obedience to your conscience you take your proper place by your brother Jesus' side as spiritual royalty and are by divine inheritance no longer bound to the everyday limitations that the rest of the world lives under.

BEING YOUR BEST
You can also improve your alignment with God's perfect frequency by being your best. This is simple. Just be the best person you can be at all times. Go forth each day on a mission of good. A cheerful attitude is contagious and it spreads, much like the ripple effect that a pebble has on the water. Be one-hundred percent committed to the highest good and happiness of yourself and others. Whatever good wishes you put

out into the universe will come back to you multiplied many times over in the end. You have probably heard the saying, "What goes around, comes around." Well it goes for good things as well!

- Desire only good for all concerned.
- Operate from integrity at all times.
- Keep your commitments.
- Do what you say you are going to do when you say you are going to do it.
- Respect others and their time.
- Honor all your appointments.
- Be on time.
- Be a courteous driver.
- Help others when the opportunity presents itself.
- Be honest.
- Do not judge others; accept others just the way they are.
- Apologize when you're wrong.
- Always do the right thing.
- Always look your best.
- Smile.
- Be thankful.
- Be polite.
- Be considerate.
- Do not whine and complain.
- Do not criticize.
- Do not gossip.
- Spread joy in the world!

DON'T COMPLAIN!

Whenever you think or complain about your negative circumstances; your poor work conditions, lack of money, or unhappy relationships, etc., you are providing a "current" image for God's creative power to project. God's creative power cannot tell the difference between a past, current or future image. It just takes whatever you are presently focusing on as the current image to project. So, what this means is that the more you think and complain about your past and present unwanted circumstances, the more you will project what you don't want into your future.

MAINTAIN A CHEERFUL STATE OF MIND

Maintain a peaceful, happy, relaxed, loving, faithful state of mind to remain in the "miracle zone." Watch only positive programming on television and at the movies. Read uplifting books and articles. Fill your mind with positive food every chance you get. Talk only about good things and don't complain. Take time to de-stress your mind and body with soothing hot baths or long relaxing walks.

BE CAREFUL OF YOUR ASSOCIATIONS

Many who have never relinquished themselves to a total commitment to good, lack the "sensitized" conscience that would prevent them from using or harming others and are people you should probably avoid.

It is this lack of commitment for good/God, that every individual must make for themselves at some point, that is the true root of all evil. Without this commitment to good, there is nothing to prevent these dark self-serving souls from doing whatever it takes to meet their own needs, without ever really being considerate of anyone else's feelings, happiness or success but their own. Medically, this condition is known as "narcissistic personality disorder" (more about this disorder can be found on the web).

To drown out the emptiness and unfulfillment of their life, which results from their own selfishness, lack of empathy, lack of appreciation and negative actions, these individuals will usually (but not always) delve into some form of self-pleasure to fill the void, overindulging in alcohol, drugs, partying, pornography, food, body image obsession, affairs, sports, gambling, ambition, working out, the internet, computer games, shopping or sex. Another interesting characteristic of the narcissist, is that they seem to never recognize themselves as being one.

If you come into contact with people who fit this description, I highly recommend that you avoid relationships and dealings with them like the plague because not only will they continually mock your commitment to good, they will probably end up hurting you, taking more from you in the relationship than they will ever give back, will pull you down to their level, or use you heartlessly in the end with no remorse. In this, I am not saying not to forgive them and love them unconditionally, just to do so at a safe distance. Scripture reference: "Give not that which is holy unto the dogs, neither cast your pearls before swine, less they trample them under their feet and turn again and rend you." (St. Matthew 7:6)

BEWARE OF ANY TEACHING THAT PROFESSES THAT THERE IS NO SUCH THING AS GOOD AND EVIL OR RIGHT AND WRONG

If there was really no such thing as evil then why does the Lord 's Prayer, given to us by Jesus the "all-knowing" master Himself, tell us to pray to be delivered from evil, if evil does not truly exist? Unfortunately, when a person refuses to acknowledge the existence of evil, they won't pray to be protected from it, which of course would leave them completely vulnerable to it. Sorry to say, but this way of thinking is like an ostrich that has its head buried in the sand in the middle of a busy road!

As far as the other erroneous teaching that says there is no such thing as right and wrong goes, it has only gained popularity because it allows those who want to live according to their own rules (regardless of what their conscience is telling them to do), the free rein to continue to do so. Voila! With this new philosophy, these souls are completely free to do anything they choose to without being held accountable to the pain their selfishness and thoughtless actions causes others. "Hey, I'm not responsible for their feelings anyway! It's all good!" Spoken like a true narcissist, I'll tell you! This teaching not only ends up hurting others, but it also directs these poor misguided souls away from the alignment that would give them full access to God's supernatural power, meaning that their level of demonstration will always remain immature and drastically limited. But you won't be able to tell these egoists this, because they get puffed up with pride over even the smallest demonstrations...like up front parking places! The scriptures put it this way, "For everyone that doeth evil hateth the light, neither cometh to the light, lest his deeds should be reproved." (John 3:20) This scripture tells us that those who only care about doing what they want to do, don't want to have their negative actions highlighted or recognized as being wrong.

The truth is...the base line of right and wrong is exactly the same for everyone who is sensitized to their conscience. Meaning that we don't really need anyone to tell us that to hurt others, ourselves or our Heavenly Father, whether that be through infidelity, fornication, lying, cheating, stealing or killing is wrong, we know this instinctively if we will only listen with true sincerity to our conscience. But many, to their own great misfortune, don't want to listen or do the right thing, thereby effectively cutting themselves off from having full access to supernatural power!

For those who think that their sins are more fun than accessing supernatural power, you couldn't be more mistaken. I will tell you, I have been known to sin with the best of them. But, there isn't one sin, whether it be drugs, fornication, excess drinking, etc., that could ever come close to the joyous feeling of making a quantum leap and living your wildest dreams; with dreams that materialized effortlessly and instantaneously right before your very eyes! "Repent: for the kingdom of heaven is at hand! " (Matthew 4:17)

As a special side note: We are all our brother's keepers and those who are truly on the path to spiritual enlightenment are extremely conscientious of the positive and negative effects their words, deeds and actions have in the world and would never choose to hurt others for their own selfish gain...ever!

APPLICATION IS CRITICAL
The optimum frequency for alignment is achieved through the mastery of each of the exercises contained in Step Two. As previously mentioned, alignment is like tuning in a radio station. Being even slightly off the mark can greatly affects the clarity of the signal, right? But once perfect alignment is attained you have full power at your complete disposal and can decree whatever you want into your life or the lives of your loved ones or make a quantum leap. At full power, you will have real power behind your words. You will have the ability to speak that mountain of debt out of your life, to command prosperity to come into your life to bless you and others, to order sickness and disease to leave the infirm, to decree a windfall of success in your business, to order the right relationship to come into your life and any other good thing you would like to do. "Thou shall also *decree* a thing, and it shall be established unto thee: and the light shall shine upon thy ways." (Job 22:28) In the Webster's dictionary, the word decree means: to order or command by someone in authority. While you are in perfect align-

ment, according to the scriptures, you inherit the authority to decree or declare any good thing done for yourself and others! Do not be afraid to stand up and claim the authority that is yours by God's divine ordinance while you are in perfect alignment! Because when you hold back or shrink from the God-given authority that is rightfully yours to claim and exercise, you will not be of any good to yourself or others.

Aligned—unrestricted access to infinite supernatural creative power to use in any positive, beneficial way you choose for your good and the good of others.

Not aligned—no access

The step of alignment is critical to your success and must be applied consistently. Make the full commitment now. Be willing to do whatever is necessary. It may help to create cards that will remind you of the disciplines of this step that you are working on. *Follow the system in its entirety and you shall succeed.* If you fail to fully understand and master Step Two you can severely restrict your success, causing it to take so long that you will lose interest before achieving any measurable results. Special note: You do not have to complete step II to proceed ahead. Just do your best to take possitive action toward mastering this step everyday.

STEP THREE

PROGRAMMING THE NEW LIFEPRINT

In Step III you will be analyzing your past, designing the new lifeprint for your future and learning the steps to program it in your subconscious mind.

CURRENT REALITY PRODUCED FROM PAST BELIEFS

Examining your past is required foundational work for Step Three. Your reality has been constructed from all the prior beliefs that you have bought into about yourself and your life. As in the construction of a building, one starts with a blueprint from which the building emerges. Your beliefs were the blueprint for your life or your lifeprint. Your finished life is an exact image of the original lifeprint. If the original blueprint for a building is lost, it is not difficult for an architect to recreate a new one. He would simply look at the finished building and then reconstruct a blueprint from the finished product. The same process can be used in the reconstruction of an accurate lifeprint for your life. If you want to know what your lifeprint has been, then look at the life you have constructed. The life you have lived is a perfect representation of your past mental lifeprint.

"Your range of available choices, right now, is limitless."
Carl Frederick

OLD BELIEFS ARE FIXED SELF-FULFILLING PROPHESIES

When beliefs, no matter how subtle, are initially bought into in child-hood they are picked up and projected into reality through the immutable natural laws of God we live under. With each projection these beliefs became more and more firmly entrenched in your subconscious mind, eventually becoming fixed self-fulfilling prophesies. This means that early beliefs like, "I'm not as smart as the other kids," "I'm so clumsy," "Nobody likes me," "I never get picked first," along with the beliefs that come later in life like, " I'm always late," "I can't seem to get ahead financially," "I'm an unlucky person," "Life isn't fair," eventually become patterned experiences that happen to us throughout the course of our lives. These beliefs or slides are locked into the cartridge of the mental slide projector and as the subconscious cartridge revolves, they are projected repeatedly, being validated and reinforced, thus creating unwanted patterns and glass ceilings. This will explain why that, just when you are starting to get ahead in your finances, your weight loss program, your career, your relationships or your happiness, that something always seems to happen to sabotage you. The setbacks that plague you, whether they be financial, emotional, spiritual or physical, are not happening by accident. They are happening by design and specifically occur to protect your current limiting beliefs.

If your life were a soap opera it would be called "As the Cartridge Turns!" The beliefs fixed in your subconscious mind will continue to pop-up and play over and over, and will continue to do so until they are changed.

This natural process of belief reinforcement explains why so many women who have been physically or mentally abused, continue to attract abusive relationships into their lives, one after another. These women have a self-destructive pattern that has become fixed in their subconscious minds. A negative pattern which is being automatically played out for them again and again by God's impersonal creative mechanism. The source of the on-going negative pattern could be a belief that, "men hurt me" or "I am not worthy of a happy relationship." Such negative beliefs are usually formed in childhood as a result of an abusive or unloving father, sexual abuse by a family member or friend, sibling rivalry or a myriad of other causes. Fortunately, the cause of the offending slide does not need to be identified in order for it to be successfully reprogrammed. This is a good thing, because the originating cause of a bad slide may never be identified. Still, the offending slide must be sought out and reprogrammed or it will continue to relentlessly cycle and project. Deprogramming of a negative slide can be as simple as deciding that you no longer accept that particular belief or as complicated as speaking literally thousands of reprogramming affirmations. Whatever it takes it is a small price to pay to eradicate the negative beliefs that have been causing all the pain and grief in your life.

IDENTIFYING THE UNDESIRABLE, LIMITING CHARACTERISTICS OF YOUR OLD LIFEPRINT

In the Self Analysis Exercise, you will be identifying your "bad slides" or undesirable beliefs that you will want to reprogram. This exercise is based on a very simple premise. By identifying the negative things that have happened in your past, you will simultaneously be identifying your bad slides.

Read the analysis statements on the following pages and fill in the blanks. A few thought-provoking examples have been provided for you in each category.

ANALYSIS EXERCISE

PERSONALITY
In my past, I have projected undesirable personality characteristics, such as:

_____

_____

_____

_____

_____

But they are no longer true for me!

Personality Examples:
Fear, Lack of Self-Confidence, Jealousy, Procrastination, Judgment, Temper, Bad Attitude, Impatience, Stress, Worry, Mental Turmoil, Prejudice, Resentment, Non-Communication ...

PHYSICAL
In my past, I have projected undesirable physical characteristics, such as:

_____

_____

_____

_____

_____

But they are no longer true for me!

Physical Examples:
Excess Weight, Lack of Exercise, Low Energy Level, Poor Eating Habits, Sweets, Over Eating, Back Problems, Poor Muscle Tone, Bad Complexion, Unhealthy Mouth, Disease (be specific)...

RELATIONSHIPS — MATE
In my past, I have projected undesirable characteristics
with my mate, such as:

_____

_____

_____

_____

_____

But they are no longer true for me!

Relationships — Mate Examples:
Lack of Love, Physical Incompatibility, Jealousy, Financial
Problems, Arguing, Mental Abuse, Physical Abuse, Lack of
Communication, Lack of Respect, Lack of Loyalty, Lack of
Consideration, Drug and/or Alcohol Abuse...

RELATIONSHIPS — FRIENDS
In my past, I have projected undesirable characteristics in my
friendships, such as:

_____

_____

_____

_____

_____

But they are no longer true for me!

Relationships — Friends Examples:
Friends Who Take Advantage, Fairweather Friends, Not
Enough Time With Your Friends, Imbalance In Friends,
Lack of Support...

RELATIONSHIPS—FAMILY

In my past, I have projected undesirable characteristics in my family such as:

_____

_____

_____

_____

_____

But they are no longer true for me!

Relationship — Family Examples:
Lack of respect, Not Enough Quality Time, Arguing, Mental Abuse, Lack of Support, Lack of Communication...

FINANCIAL

In my past, I have projected undesirable financial characteristics, such as:

_____

_____

_____

_____

But they are no longer true for me!

Financial Examples:
Lack of Money, Instability, Tax Problems, Over-Spending, Poor Bookkeeping, Debt, Being Taken Advantage of, Lack of Savings, Taking Advantage of Others...

CAREER

In my past, I have projected undesirable career characteristics, such as:

_____

_____

_____

_____

_____

But they are no longer true for me!

Career Examples:
Unfulfillment, Problems with Management, Problems with Co-Workers, Inadequate Pay, Disorganization, Lack of Motivation, Bad Hours, Gossip, Prejudice, No Growth Potential ....

MATERIAL

In my past, I have projected undesirable material characteristics, such as:

_____

_____

_____

_____

_____

But they are no longer true for me!

Material Examples:
Settling for Second Best, Poor Quality, Used, Poor Choices ...

SELECTING YOUR NEW SLIDE REPLACEMENTS

The undesirable characteristics you have now identified in these eight major areas of your life represent your bad slides that will need to be reprogrammed. These slides are the source of the undesirable results or situations you have been experiencing throughout your life. The goal is to now find the right reprogramming affirmations to reverse them. These new affirmations will give you the new beliefs that will need to be programmed into your subconscious mind to replace all of the old negative patterns. The reversal selection process is simple. For example, if you are a procrastinator, then from the list of pre-written positive affirmations listed later in this chapter, you would choose the affirmation, "In my new lifeprint I do things when they should be done without hesitation." This affirmation represents the exact opposite of the offending negative belief that needs to be replaced.

REPROGRAMMING TAKES TIME

Reprogramming may not happen overnight. And before the new beliefs have become deeply entrenched into your subconscious mind, you will still continue to have negative experiences or what I call "leftovers." Getting upset about these leftovers when they happen to you will only serve to reinstate them and give them a new foothold. The best thing for you to do when "leftovers" happen is to not to react at all. Remain calm and remind yourself that reprogramming takes time. Many of these negative beliefs have been a part of you for a very long time and it may take multiple repetitions of your new positive affirmations to effectively reprogram those old beliefs. Here's what to do…whenever you have an unpleasant "leftover" or bad experience, *instead* of allowing yourself to become upset, remain absolutely calm, immediately recognize yourself as the source, and then transmute any anger into conviction as you recite a full denial affirmation specifically related to that event. "I used to attract people who took advantage of me, but that is no longer true for me! I NOW attract people who create healthy, win-win situations in my life!"

RELEASING ATTACHMENT TO GENERAL NEGATIVE BELIEFS

Every event that happens in your life must happen through your realm of possibility. Your realm of possibility is what you accept as being possible in your life. Humanity's framework of "generally accepted beliefs," are beliefs that you don't have to buy into if you don't want to. Some of these generally accepted negative beliefs are:

"Whenever I wash my car it rains."

"You have your good days and your bad days."

"Accidents just happen."

"You have to take the bad with the good."

"You can't have everything."

"Bad things come in threes."

"The good always die young."

"You can't be happy all the time."

"You can't win them all."

You do not have to buy into these negative, limiting belief patterns if you do not choose to. Make a firm decision within yourself now, not to continue to accept these negative beliefs as being true for you. Because absolutely nothing is impossible, you have the ability to remove anything you want to from your realm of possibility. So why not choose to create new belief parameters that only allow for a long-life filled with harmony, love, health, happiness, good fortune and prosperity; deprogramming any possibility for accidents, cancer, and all other forms of illness for you and your loved ones? Don't think it's possible? Then you need to do a little more work on step number one, because anything is possible!

SELECTING YOUR NEW BLUEPRINT
Now that you have analyzed your past, you can begin to design the new lifeprint for your future. We will accomplish this by first learning the proper guidelines for goal setting.

YOU ARE IN CHARGE
First of all you are in charge. This is your life. Do not allow yourself to be overly influenced by your parents, friends, business associates, peers or society in general. The decisions you make about your life are yours alone to make. You're the one that is going to have to live with them, right? But, at the same time you should not be selfish. In making your decisions, you should be very conscientious and respectful of the feelings of others who are in your life because they will also be affected. This is about balance and should not cross the line into either being

a self-serving narcissist or the other extreme of being the proverbial doormat. For example, if you are married with children it would be very wrong to make choices that do not take your family into full consideration. However, if you are not attached and want to do anything, from living on the beach in a grass hut selling T-shirts, to living an opulent life of "the rich and famous," then that is your business. So long as what you decide to do is legal, moral and ethical, will bless others and is in alignment with your Heavenly Father's will...then go for it! Your life choices are ultimately up to you and you're the one that will have to live with them and be judged for them in the end.

DECIDE WHAT YOU WANT

Personal success can only be realized when you focus on what will make you happy, so long as your success does not infringe on the happiness of others or your Heavenly Father's will. It is up to you to decide what you want out of life. When the goals you choose include what will be for your highest good as well as others and are in alignment with your Heavenly Father's will of good for everyone, you will know that you have made good selections! By the way, if you are unsure what direction to take at this point don't worry, because you can always ask for guidance from infinite intelligence or use some of the thought provoking affirmations that are provided ahead on pages 134-145 to get your mental juices flowing. These pre-written affirmations will give you numerous ideas to ponder, ideas that you might not have otherwise thought of that can help you decide. If your past goals have always revolved around everybody else's idea of success for you but your own, then you have probably never asked yourself the question, "What do I really want out of life?" If this has been the case, is it any wonder why you don't know what it is that you want right now? If the life choices you have made so far have been running through the filter of what others want or will think, maybe it's time for you to start asking yourself what you want. With the sky being the limit, whatever your heart desires is possible for you to achieve.

HOW BIG CAN YOU BELIEVE?

If you can conceive it in your mind, it is possible. Ask yourself this, "If nothing is impossible for God's creative process to achieve in my life, then what do I really want, that will be of benefit me and others?" The list you come up with may be incredible, but if you can believe it…it will be possible for you to attain! The question is, how big can you believe?

START WHERE YOU CAN AND GROW FROM THERE

Start where you can, and master that level of belief and accomplishment first. Achieving even small results will validate the limitless ability of God's power to create the life you want. With consistent results you will slowly expand your ability to believe for bigger and better things. For example, you should not start with a goal of $1,000,000 or more, unless you can honestly believe that big at this point in time. Now, if you can believe that big then GO FOR IT! But, if you can't, then it would be fruitless to start with a monetary goal you can't believe in for yourself. Start where you can, perhaps it is $50,000 or a $100,000. Believe for that goal and once it has been attained you can set new, higher ones if you wish. Remember this is not your only chance! This is only the beginning of an ongoing process that once mastered, will always be there for you to use again and again for the rest of your life. Not only for your benefit, but for the incredible benefit you can be to many others as well.

WE ALL DEVELOP AT DIFFERENT RATES

Through your new experiences you will eventually learn to trust the process completely and your confidence will grow stronger and stronger. Don't worry about your rate of ascent because we all develop mastery at different rates. People who are naturally optimistic, for example, will typically master the process much faster than the pessimistic types. This is because the optimist has a much easier time believing in extraordinary possibilities and believing that things are going to happen. Pessimistic personality types, who have developed the habit of never overextending their expectations, naturally want to see results before they will believe. Unfortunately, with this process, you have to believe it first or there will be no results! Pessimistic personality types will just have to build their belief in the process slowly, one small step at a time. This can be achieved by testing the process on small goals and observing the consistency of the results.

If you are new to this, your belief "muscle" has probably never been exercised and may be weak at first. But even if you do not get immediate results do not give up. If you will remain consistent with your efforts, results will eventually happen. They have to…it is the law! Persistence will eventually prevail and you can count on that. The proof you will derive through results will help you gain strength in your belief muscle and you'll be able to trust in God's natural laws for bigger and better things.

NO DIFFERENCE IN DEGREE OF DIFFICULTY

Before you decide how big you can believe, you should be aware that it is just as easy for God's creative power to project a beautiful mansion, as it is a cabin. For God's infinite creative source, the degree of difficulty to produce a big item is no more difficult than it is to produce a small one. We actually assign the degree of difficulty through our own pre-conceived beliefs. If we hold the *belief that* it will be more difficult for example, our belief will *cause* it more difficult. Our every belief, no matter how subtle, is being picked up by God's creative mechanism and validated for us. This is an inescapable fact of the law. In light of this, you must be very careful to release the idea of "difficulty" because everything is effortless for God's creative mechanism if we will *let* it be. Just let go of "how," align, believe, relax and let it happen.

END-RESULT GOAL SETTING

The creative mechanism only works toward end-result goals. Like a heat-seeking missile it will automatically speed toward a target that has been pre-designated by you, in this case your new lifeprint. Do not jam the missile by trying to direct it or steer it yourself. The parts you are supposed to play are simple, decide on your new lifeprint, relax, align and believe that God's unfailing Law of Cause and Effect is bringing it to fruition. Do not try to figure out *how* it is going to happen! It is not your job to figure out the middle part, between where you are now and your final destination. The middle part is none of your business! Give God's infinite all-knowing power the freedom to direct your path to your goals and it will automatically put you on the most perfect course possible, because that is exactly what you are asking it to do. When you allow your limited conscious mind to interfere by trying to figure out what the best means would be for you, you jam the missile and limit the best and most immediate path that God's creative mechanism could produce for you from being created. By allowing yourself to think for example that, "The lottery is probably the only way this could possibly happen," limits what could have been 100,000 other better ways that your goals could have come to fruition! Simply set your goals and start trusting that you are on the best path possible and God's law will automatically put you on the best possible course to your destination, and if God's perfect path is for you to win the lottery then that is what will happen!

ACTION

You will be required to take action along the way. And as God's creative power lays out your best course for you, you will have to be one-hundred percent willing to follow whatever steps that are presented for you to do. How will you know what these steps are? Your heart will tell you if you will just tune-in and listen carefully for guidance. This means that you will just know! Fortunately, in addition to the perfect path, God's creative power will also provide you with all the motivation and courage necessary to do the work presented. Failure to follow through at any stage of the path will block your results. More will be discussed on this important step later in Step Seven.

ASKING FOR THE UNKNOWN

Just ahead you will be selecting your end-result goals for the eight major areas of your life. In most instances you will know exactly what you want. But in some cases, even with the suggestions provided, you may not. For example, if you want a new job but have no idea what your perfect work would be, then you would simply ask for the "ideal job for me." This will work just fine because infinite intelligence, which is part of God's power, knows everything about you and knows what that ideal job would be and the perfect way to put it in your path. So, if you are not sure, simply allow infinite intelligence to fill-in the perfect solutions for you. However, you may be able to set some known parameters for yourself such as; the ideal job making over $60,000 a year, with a great boss, working in a beautiful environment with my own spacious office, advancement potential, doing work I love, with people I love to work with. It is possible for you to set general parameters and then let infinite intelligence fill in the rest if that is what you would like to do.

PRIVACY

After you have selected your goals, it is extremely important that you keep them private. Without meaning to, others who may lack faith in you or in the abilities of God's natural laws could have a very negative effect on your dreams with their thoughts and attitudes. The negative thoughts and attitudes they put out are like killer-missiles that shoot down your dreams! You can almost feel your dreams being deflated as you tell these dream-robbers of your plans. Protect your dreams by only sharing them with people you are absolutely sure can believe in you and in God's infinite possibilities.

MINDING YOUR OWN BUSINESS

Don't ever impose your will on the lives of others unless you are *sure* it is welcome. Imposing your will over the will of another person is wrong. Two prime examples of this would be, parents telling their children what they are going to be when they grow up and people who decide who they want to marry without the other person's consent. This is in direct violation of another person's free will and is manipulative, selfish and controlling and is something that should never be done.

TIME-FRAME

In this spiritual process, we do not set specific dates. Why? Date setting actually hinders the process from working at its optimum level and in the most expedient way that it can. What could possibly be faster than the most expedient way possible? What you might think would take a minimum of a year, God's creative mechanism, unhindered, could supernaturally bring forth in a week! This is why it is critical that you not put any limitations on the process with dates. Leave the perfect time-frame up to God's infinite intelligence and it will work out the perfect solution for you, in the most perfect way and time.

SIMPLIFYING YOUR FOCUS

It is important that you only work on a few end-result goals at a time, so you don't overwhelm your system. When overwhelmed, you lose your ability to focus intensely and your system does not function effectively. Focus your mind on key goals, so you do not overwhelm yourself. Focusing is like using a magnifying glass. When sunlight is focused through a magnifying glass, it produces a concentrated beam of energy.

The same effect is desired in the mental projection process. The fewer the items, the better you will be able to focus your mental energy. To assure proper focus, you should select no more than eight affirmations per category.

You may choose from the pre-written examples that have been provided, or write your own. The first selections you make should reverse each of the negative characteristics you have in each category. Refer to your undesirable characteristics listed in your "Self-Analysis Exercise" as a guide. Example: if you have a problem with your temper you would select "In my new lifeprint I now remain calm and in control, regardless of the situation" which would be the exact opposite of that negative characteristic. You may want to alter the wording of these pre-written examples to suit you, combine affirmations or custom-write your own if an appropriate affirmation is not listed and that's fine. Just be sure to be careful of your wording, because every single word matters. For example if your goal is to attract money and you say, "I now attract large sums of money to me," you may attract a brinks truck at a red light! Not exactly what you had in mind, right? Instead, you should say "I now attract large sums of money to me for my own personal use." Be sure to keep your selections to a maximum of eight per category and be sure that all your negative characteristics have been reversed before making any other selections. If you have more than eight negative characteristics to reverse, then prioritize and handle the worst of them first. As goals are accomplished you will delete them and add new ones. Remember that this is an ongoing process.

Follow these instructions very carefully!

YOUR CUT-OUT FOCUS BOOKLET KIT
In the back of this book starting on page 215, is a cut-out kit for you to make your own focus booklet. This booklet is where you will be transferring the selections you will be making just ahead. The booklet is a crucial tool in the *Seven Step* program. You will be using it daily. Before proceeding any further, **you should put your focus booklet together now**, so that it will be ready for you to transfer your selections into as you make them.

After you have made all of your selections (eight or less per category), transfer them to your daily focus booklet.

PERSONALITY

- In my new lifeprint God _now_ watches over me, perfects me, guides me, protects me and blesses me in every aspect of my life.
- In my new lifeprint I _now_ live a life where I am an open channel of goodness in the world.
- In my new lifeprint I am _now_ a patient, interested listener.
- In my new lifeprint I am _now_ a talented conversationalist and speaker.
- In my new lifeprint I _now_ attract only wonderful people into my life.
- In my new lifeprint I _now_ live a life filled with abundant over-flowing love, harmony and joy.
- In my new lifeprint I _now_ enjoy the beauty and goodness that surround me.
- In my new lifeprint I _now_ maintain only pure and clean thoughts.
- In my new lifeprint I _now_ live a life dedicated to goodness.
- In my new lifeprint I _now_ maintain peace of mind in every situation.
- In my new lifeprint I _now_ remain calm and in control, regardless of the situation.
- In my new lifeprint I _now_ treat myself with respect.
- In my new lifeprint I am _now_ happy all the time and my happiness lifts the spirits of everyone around me.
- In my new lifeprint I am _now_ cleansed of all unhealthy habits and live the wholesome, happy life I want to live.
- In my new lifeprint I _now_ leave my past in the past and freely allow myself to move ahead and live the good life I long for.
- In my new lifeprint I _now_ speak clearly and distinctly, in a relaxed, well-received manner.
- In my new lifeprint I _now_ do what it takes to create the life I desire without hesitation.
- In my new lifeprint I _now_ look for the blessing in every event.
- In my new lifeprint I am _now_ solid and steady.
- In my new lifeprint I _now_ express boundless enthusiasm and joy in my life.

- In my new lifeprint I _now_ possess a pleasing personality and I am well liked.
- In my new lifeprint I _now_ accept and love others unconditionally.
- In my new lifeprint I _now_ live a meaningful, fulfilling life.
- In my new lifeprint I _now_ live a life filled with harmony that flows peacefully.
- In my new lifeprint I am _now_ filled with creative ideas that benefit me and others.
- In my new lifeprint I am _now_ well-mannered at all times.
- In my new lifeprint I am _now_ growing spiritually and becoming more and more in touch with that part of my life.
- In my new lifeprint I _now_ experience abundant laughter, fun and joy in my life.
- In my new lifeprint I _now_ am guided, protected and blessed by God in every area of my life.
- In my new lifeprint I _now_ have divine wisdom.
- In my new lifeprint I _now_ have a great sense of humor, laughing easily and often.
- In my new lifeprint I _now_ stay on task until the things I need to do are done.
- In my new lifeprint I _now_ easily access the knowledge I need to succeed.
- In my new lifeprint I am _now_ a genius.
- In my new lifeprint I _now_ love to learn and I learn easily.
- In my new lifeprint I _now_ live a life that flows and works perfectly, freely providing me everything I need to be happy.
- In my new lifeprint I _now_ do things when they should be done without hesitation.
- In my new lifeprint my memory _now_ grows stronger every day.
- In my new lifeprint I _now_ have a sunny disposition that I share with others.
- In my new lifeprint I _now_ live a life where I am relaxed and free of stress.
- In my new lifeprint I _now_ accept people from all nationalities and respect their cultural differences.
- In my new lifeprint I _now_ live my dreams.
- In my new lifeprint I _now_ feel strong and confident in everything I do.

- In my new lifeprint I _now_ attract only that which is good and uplifting, and I am protected from that which is dark and unpleasant.

PHYSICAL

- In my new lifeprint I _now_ enjoy perfect health in my mind and body now and always.
- In my new lifeprint I _now_ love myself and my body and always do what is best for me.
- In my new lifeprint I _now_ enjoy my ideal weight of _____ pounds and easily maintain it.
- In my new lifeprint I _now_ maintain a well-groomed appearance.
- In my new lifeprint my skin is _now_ clear and youthful with a radiant appearance.
- In my new lifeprint I _now_ enjoy 20/20 vision with eyes that sparkle.
- In my new lifeprint I _now_ have a healthy mouth and a beautiful
bright smile.
- In my new lifeprint I _now_ desire pure clean water over other beverages and drink plenty every day.
- In my new lifeprint I am _now_ filled with unlimited energy.
- In my new lifeprint I _now_ live a long, healthy, happy life.
- In my new lifeprint working out is _now_ a part of my daily life.
- In my new lifeprint I _now_ eat a healthy diet everyday.
- In my new lifeprint I _now_ have a great figure that is admired by others.
- In my new lifeprint I am _now_ considered beautiful by others.
- In my new lifeprint I am _now_ considered handsome by others.
- In my new lifeprint my stomach is _now_ flat and strong.
- In my new lifeprint I _now_ look and feel younger and younger as
time goes by.
- In my new lifeprint I am _now_ flexible, strong and agile.
- In my new lifeprint I _now_ have a strong and healthy back which
supports me comfortably.

- In my new lifeprint I _now_ have a body that functions in perfect harmony and at its highest level.
- In my new lifeprint I _now_ only desire foods that will provide me with vitality and health, and I eat them in the right quantities.
- In my new lifeprint I _now_ have a firm, sexy body that is full of vibrant energy.
- In my new lifeprint I _now_ enjoy perfect, healthy sexual function.
- In my new lifeprint I _now_ have a loving, healthy sexual desire for my mate, and I am faithful to my mate in every way.
- In my new lifeprint I _now_ feel great every day for the rest of my life.
- In my new lifeprint I _now_ exercise every day in the best and most enjoyable way for me!
- In my new lifeprint I _now_ breathe easily and deeply.
- In my new lifeprint I am _now_ divinely and miraculously healed.
- In my new lifeprint I _now_ leave food on my plate when I have had enough to eat.
- In my new lifeprint I _now_ prefer and choose to eat healthy foods over unhealthy foods.
- In my new lifeprint I _now_ eat slowly and chew my food thoroughly.
- In my new lifeprint I _now_ choose raw fruits and vegetables for snacks.
- In my new lifeprint I _now_ lose weight easily down to my desired weight and maintain it.
- In my new lifeprint I _now_ allow positive changes in my eating and exercise habits, and I maintain them.
- In my new lifeprint I _now_ easily make positive behavioral changes in myself that become permanent.

RELATIONSHIPS — FRIENDS
- In my new lifeprint I _now_ enjoy many fulfilling, wonderful friendships in my life.
- In my new lifeprint all of my friends are _now_ divinely protected and miraculously blessed with whatever they need to be

truly happy now and always.
- In my new lifeprint I _now_ draw only wonderful people to me.
- In my new lifeprint I _now_ empower my friends to achieve their highest good.
- In my new lifeprint I _now_ experience many wonderful close, deep, loving, enduring, fun and meaningful relationships.
- In my new lifeprint my friends and I _now_ have fun, adventure and excitement in our time together.
- In my new lifeprint my friends _now_ hold me in high regard.
- In my new lifeprint my friends are _now_ thoughtful of me, always making my life very special.
- In my new lifeprint I am _now_ a loving, faithful friend.
- In my new lifeprint I _now_ help others become successful.
- In my new lifeprint I _now_ support others in positive ways.
- In my new lifeprint I _now_ am a leader.
- In my new lifeprint I _now_ am esteemed and respected by all.
- In my new lifeprint I _now_ have balanced healthy friendships.
- In my new lifeprint I _now_ experience a lifestyle that allows me an abundance of quality time that I enjoy with my friends.

RELATIONSHIPS — FAMILY
- In my new lifeprint all of my family is _now_ divinely protected and miraculously blessed with whatever they need to be truly happy now and always.
- In my new lifeprint I _now_ experience harmonious and loving relationships with of all my family members.
- In my new lifeprint I _now_ hold the happiness and well-being of every one of my family members in my thoughts daily.
- In my new lifeprint I _now_ bless each of my family members with protection, love, health, prosperity and happiness every day.
- In my new lifeprint I _now_ am committed and loyal to my family.
- In my new lifeprint I _now_ am an outstanding parent.
- In my new lifeprint I _now_ am always patient and loving with my family.
- In my new lifeprint all of my children are _now_ divinely protected and miraculously blessed with whatever they need to be truly happy now and always.

RELATIONSHIPS — MATE (HEALING EXISTING MARRIAGE)

- In my new lifeprint I _now_ love my husband/wife unconditionally and accept all his/her shortcomings.
- In my new lifeprint I am _now_ happily married to my husband/wife.
- In my new lifeprint we _now_ experience the highest quality marriage.
- In my new lifeprint we _now_ enjoy the same spiritual beliefs.
- In my new lifeprint we _now_ appreciate and respect our spiritual differences.
- In my new lifeprint we _now_ enjoy the same kind of recreation together.
- In my new lifeprint we _now_ allow one another space for our different recreational activities with a healthy balance of quality time for the family.
- In my new lifeprint we _now_ trust one another completely with no fear.
- In my new lifeprint our marriage is _now_ balanced and healthy for us both.
- In my new lifeprint our marriage is _now_ strong and lasts a lifetime.
- In my new lifeprint we are _now_ filled with love for one another.
- In my new lifeprint we _now_ have open communication in all situations.
- In my new lifeprint we _now_ support one another for our highest good.
- In my new lifeprint we _now_ allow one another independence.
- In my new lifeprint we are _now_ completely loyal to one another.
- In my new lifeprint we are _now_ considerate of one another.
- In my new lifeprint we are _now_ totally committed to one another.
- In my new lifeprint we _now_ communicate our needs gently to each other.
- In my new lifeprint we _now_ successfully meet one another's needs to our mutual satisfaction.
- In my new lifeprint we _now_ find one another mutually attractive.

- In my new lifeprint we are _now_ stable, happy and comfortable financially.
- In my new lifeprint this relationship _now_ successfully flows with change, adjusting easily.
- In my new lifeprint we _now_ realize that we are perfect for each other in absolutely every way.
- In my new lifeprint we _now_ mutually contribute financially with a joint annual income of over _____.
- In my new lifeprint we _now_ live in mutually fulfilling and immensely satisfying bliss for the rest of our long, healthy, joyous lives.
- In my new lifeprint this relationship is _now_ blessed and protected now and always.
- In my new lifeprint we _now_ have an emotionally fulfilling relationship.
- In my new lifeprint we _now_ have a physically fulfilling relationship for both of us.
- In my new lifeprint we _now_ mutually support and empower one another.
- In my new lifeprint we are _now_ kind to one another.
- In my new lifeprint we _now_ respect one another.
- In my new lifeprint we _now_ enjoy one another.
- In my new lifeprint we _now_ enjoy plenty of relaxing fun time together.
- In my new lifeprint our children _now_ enhance our happiness together.
- In my new lifeprint we _now_ live our life alcohol and drug free.
- In my new lifeprint we are _now_ happy nonsmokers.
- In my new lifeprint we _now_ live long, healthy lives together.
- In my new lifeprint we _now_ share the same basic values.
- In my new lifeprint we are _now_ light drinkers.
- In my new lifeprint we _now_ go to church regularly together.
- In my new lifeprint we are _now_ always able to work things out in a reasonable fashion.
- In my new lifeprint we _now_ support each other in a healthy diet and exercise program that is perfect for each of us.
- In my new lifeprint we _now_ put one another first in the relationship over everyone and everything else.

- In my new lifeprint I _now_ let down my guard and effortlessly attract my true soul-mate into my life now.
- In my new lifeprint I _now_ easily attract, meet and marry my true love/soul-mate at the perfect time for us both.
- In my new lifeprint I _now_ enjoy a very close, loving, meaningful, happy and lasting marriage that fulfills both of us in every way.
- In my new lifeprint for my perfect marriage we experience the highest quality relationship.
- In my new lifeprint for my perfect marriage we enjoy the same spiritual beliefs.
- In my new lifeprint for my perfect marriage we enjoy the same kind of recreation together.
- In my new lifeprint for my perfect marriage we trust one another completely with no fear.
- In my new lifeprint for my perfect marriage is balanced and healthy for us both.
- In my new lifeprint my perfect marriage is divinely blessed and lasts for the rest of our happy lives together.
- In my new lifeprint for my perfect marriage we are filled with love for one another.
- In my new lifeprint for my perfect marriage we have open communication in all situations.
- In my new lifeprint for my perfect marriage we support one another for our highest good.
- In my new lifeprint for my perfect marriage we allow one another independence.
- In my new lifeprint for my perfect marriage we are completely loyal to one another.
- In my new lifeprint for my perfect marriage we are considerate of one another.
- In my new lifeprint for my perfect marriage we are totally committed to one another.
- In my new lifeprint for my perfect marriage we communicate our needs gently to each other.
- In my new lifeprint for my perfect marriage we successfully meet

one another's needs to our mutual satisfaction.

- In my new lifeprint for my perfect marriage we find one another mutually attractive.
- In my new lifeprint for my perfect marriage we are stable, happy and comfortable financially.
- In my new lifeprint for my perfect marriage our marriage successfully flows with change, adjusting easily.
- In my new lifeprint for my perfect marriage we are perfect in absolutely every way for each other.
- In my new lifeprint for my perfect marriage we mutually contribute financially with a joint income of over $_____.
- In my new lifeprint for my perfect marriage we live in mutually fulfilling and immensely satisfying marital bliss for the rest of our long, healthy, joyous lives together.
- In my new lifeprint for my perfect marriage our marriage is divinely blessed and protected now and always.
- In my new lifeprint for my perfect marriage we have a beautiful, emotionally fulfilling marriage.
- In my new lifeprint for my perfect marriage we are both physically fulfilled in our marriage.
- In my new lifeprint for my perfect marriage we mutually support and empower one another.
- In my new lifeprint for my perfect marriage we are always kind to one another.
- In my new lifeprint for my perfect marriage we respect one another.
- In my new lifeprint for my perfect marriage we enjoy each others company more than the company of anyone else.
- In my new lifeprint for my perfect marriage we have fun together.
- In my new lifeprint for my perfect marriage our children enhance our happiness together.
- In my new lifeprint for my perfect marriage we live our lives alcohol and drug free.
- In my new lifeprint for my perfect marriage we are happy non-smokers.
- In my new lifeprint for my perfect marriage we live long,

healthy lives together.

- In my new lifeprint for my perfect marriage we have the same basic values and morals.
- In my new lifeprint for my perfect marriage we are light drinkers.
- In my new lifeprint for my perfect marriage we go to church regularly together.
- In my new lifeprint for my perfect marriage we are always able to work things out reasonably to our mutual satisfaction.
- In my new lifeprint for my perfect marriage we are blessed with beautiful, healthy children that grow up and lead happy, wholesome, independent, prosperous lives.
- In my new lifeprint for my perfect marriage our children are divinely protected now and always.
- In my new lifeprint for my perfect marriage we put one another first in the relationship over all else.

FINANCIAL

- In my new lifeprint I _now_ have the complete financial freedom to do, be and have anything I desire.
- In my new lifeprint I am _now_ a powerful money magnet, continuous abundance flows into my life in many miraculous ways for my own discretionary use.
- In my new lifeprint my finances are _now_ divinely blessed and protected.
- In my new lifeprint my financial situation is _now_ divinely healed. I am _now_ permanently free of debt and all other money problems.
- In my new lifeprint I _now_ have the financial ability to purchase, in cash, anything I desire.
- In my new lifeprint I _now_ have an annual income of $_____.
- In my new lifeprint I am _now_ able to give $_____ a month/week to take care of those who are less fortunate than me.
- In my new lifeprint I _now_ use my excess money to help others.
- In my new lifeprint I _now_ become more prosperous day by day.
- In my new lifeprint I _now_ have an unlimited well-spring of wealth.

- In my new lifeprint I _now_ make a fortune doing what I love.
- In my new lifeprint I _now_ attract money easily and effortlessly.
- In my new lifeprint I _now_ have perfect money handling ability.
- In my new lifeprint I _now_ give and receive freely.
- In my new lifeprint I _now_ serve many people and my income grows proportionately.
- In my new lifeprint I _now_ use my money for my highest good and the good of others.
- In my new lifeprint I _now_ use my talents wisely to make more money.
- In my new lifeprint money _now_ flows freely to me.
- In my new lifeprint I _now_ use money to benefit mankind in wonderful ways.
- In my new lifeprint I _now_ invest my money wisely.
- In my new lifeprint I _now_ am intuitive and wise regarding money.
- In my new lifeprint I _now_ enjoy financial freedom without a care in the world.
- In my new lifeprint I _now_ attract ideal opportunities to increase my wealth and take advantage of those opportunities.
- In my new lifeprint I _now_ have capable, honest people helping me with my finances.
- In my new lifeprint I _now_ easily pay my taxes in full and on time.
- In my new lifeprint I am _now_ a responsible spender, only spending what I can afford to spend.
- In my new lifeprint I am _now_ in control of my finances.

CAREER

- In my new lifeprint I _now_ have the (new) ideal career for me where I am the most benefited and of the most benefit to others.
- In my new lifeprint I _now_ always attract new ways to succeed in
  my work.
- In my new lifeprint I _now_ have the (new) perfect career to fulfill my life's purpose.
- In my new lifeprint I _now_ have the perfect (new) career.

- In my new lifeprint my job is _now_ divinely protected and secure.
- In my new lifeprint I am _now_ successful in all that I do.
- In my new lifeprint I am _now_ organized.
- In my new lifeprint I am _now_ in a career that benefits mankind and
  is fulfilling to me.
- In my new lifeprint I _now_ help many people through my work.
- In my new lifeprint I _now_ set and prioritize my goals daily.
- In my new lifeprint I _now_ am persistent; nothing stops me from achieving my career goals.
- In my new lifeprint I _now_ make the right decisions promptly, wisely and firmly.
- In my new lifeprint I _now_ attract ideal clients from expected and unexpected sources daily.
- In my new lifeprint I _now_ attract perfect opportunities to succeed and act on them.
- In my new lifeprint I _now_ achieve all my goals efficiently.
- In my new lifeprint I _now_ am focused and centered on my goals; nothing deters me.
- In my new lifeprint I _now_ persist through any challenge.
- In my new lifeprint I _now_ achieve my daily goals easily with time left over.
- In my new lifeprint I _now_ love what I do.
- In my new lifeprint I _now_ feel good about my work.
- In my new lifeprint I _now_ love to go out and achieve my goals every day.
- In my new lifeprint I _now_ always finish whatever I start.
- In my new lifeprint I _now_ love responsibility.
- In my new lifeprint I _now_ am brilliant in my work.
- In my new lifeprint I _now_ provide a service/product many people
  benefit from and I _now_ benefit greatly in the process.
- In my new lifeprint I _now_ delegate perfectly.
- In my new lifeprint I _now_ attract the perfect people to work with me.
- In my new lifeprint I _now_ am completely free to achieve any level of success I choose.

- In my new lifeprint I _now_ am motivated to succeed in my chosen work.
- In my new lifeprint I _now_ attract the perfect plan of action to be successful and act on it.
- In my new lifeprint I _now_ am filled with eagerness every morning to begin my day.
- In my new lifeprint I _now_ am completely fulfilled in my work.
- In my new lifeprint I _now_ am rewarded with abundant financial returns for my work.
- In my new lifeprint I _now_ have unlimited earning potential.
- In my new lifeprint I _now_ set my own hours.
- In my new lifeprint I _now_ work in a loving and harmonious environment.
- In my new lifeprint I _now_ am recognized and appreciated for what I do.
- In my new lifeprint I _now_ work in a career that is easy and fun.
- In my new lifeprint I _now_ have ideal offices for my work always.

MATERIAL
In my new lifeprint I _now_ own and retain for my unlimited use:
- A new house (list all the specific characteristics)
- A new wardrobe
- A boat (list all the specific characteristics)
- A new car (list characteristics)
- New furniture (describe)

In my new lifeprint I _now_ have unlimited access to (without ownership):
- A boat/yacht
- Unlimited travel
- Lake home
- Airplane

PROGRAMMING THE NEW BLUEPRINT
Your new lifeprint will be programmed through daily focus sessions. The key to eradicating old unwanted patterns and implanting your new desired lifeprint is to repeatedly feed your new self-talk statements to your conscious and subconscious minds at the same time.

This is not a complex process and is done simply by repeating the statements aloud with intense emotion. When you speak the statements aloud with emotion you are in effect filtering the statements past the conscious mind and into the deeper subconscious mind, emotion being the critical catalyst in this process.

PROGRAMMING BOTH PHASES OF MIND

It is critical that both levels of mind be programmed. Programming only the subconscious phase of mind, which is what is done in hypnosis, is usually only effective for a short term. In ninety-percent of the cases where hypnosis is used, the positive changes only last for a short while before the subject reverts back to their old negative behavior patterns. During hypnosis, the subconscious mind, which has no reality checkpoint of its own, blindly accepts whatever it is being told and then acts it out. However, once the subject is brought out of the hypnotic state, the conscious mind which was not involved in the hypnosis process, is back on duty and immediately recognizes the new behavior as inconsistent with the subject's current lifeprint and subsequently reprograms the subject's subconscious mind back to it's original lifeprint. An act it performs through internal self-talk. This explains why it is crucial to involve both the conscious and subconscious phases of mind in the reprogramming process. To successfully accomplish this you will be fully conscious and alert during your daily focus sessions versus a hypnotic state.

THE IMPORTANCE OF EMOTION

Unemotionalized repetitions have little impact on the programming of your new lifeprint. The number of repetitions required for results can be greatly reduced by mixing intense feelings and emotions with your words as you repeat them. Repetitions spoken without emotion have little impact on programming your new lifeprint into your subconscious mind. Only words wrapped in powerful conviction and emotion can reach past the conscious mind and gain access into the subconscious mind. Using intense emotion can also greatly reduce the number of repetitions you will need for successful reprogramming. In fact, it could be the difference between it taking only a few hundred self-talk affirmations compared to literally thousands!

WHY ALOUD?

The spoken word is actually the first transition of thought to form. The spoken word produces a physical vibration which begins to put the creative process into motion. Whatever you speak into the universe with emotionalized belief and conviction must return to you in its same likeness. Needless to say, the spoken word has a much more profound effect than repeating the same statement to yourself. So repeating your affirmations aloud whenever possible is best, but if the setting you are in does not allow for this, then you can repeat them under your breath.

PERSISTENCE

In reprogramming, the important thing for you is not to miss even one day of focus. It takes many, many days, even weeks of intense focus before you may see noticeable results, with each day building upon the day before. It takes time, patience and consistency to breakthrough the resistance of your existing lifeprint in your conscious mind and this can be a real test of your commitment. But if you will hold on and remain diligent with your daily efforts, you will finally break through the resistance and results will begin to happen. Once you begin to get results, the results will begin to build upon themselves. When this snowball effect finally begins to happen, and it will if you are consistent, it is no time for you to rest, let up, or coast. You will want to keep the momentum going by continuing to focus daily! A good analogy to represent what is being said here would be the start-up of a heavy locomotive on a railroad track. At the onset, even with the locomotive at full power, it doesn't move, its wheels only spin in place. Then at stage two, with full power still continuously applied, the wheels occasionally grab hold and slow forward movement begins. Then comes stage three, with the throttle still at full speed, the wheels finally begin to grab a firm hold and the train begins to gain more and more speed and momentum. The real challenge is not to stop doing the exercises on a daily basis once you get rolling. This process takes time, commitment and intensity to master, so you have to hold on, remain committed and keep going. If you don't quit out of impatience, frustration, discouragement or a lack of discipline you will certainly see results. You have to, it's the law! You don't have to worry about wasted efforts because this works every time, if you will just commit to work it!

OPTIMUM CONDITIONS FOR YOUR DAILY FOCUS EXERCISE
The best time of day to do your focus exercise is in the morning, because it puts you in the proper frame of mind for the day. Taking an early morning walk alone is a good way to perform your daily focus exercises. The act of walking or pacing (which can also be done indoors with soft music in the background) actually aids in the effectiveness of your focus exercises. The cadence of your steps helps to drive in or punctuate each word as you speak them. Walking, however, is not the only acceptable method. There is also the meditation style, which can be just as effective. If the weather is bad or you are not able to walk for some reason, you may find that you prefer the meditation style of focusing. For the meditation style of focus you will need a quiet place in your home or garden that you can escape to for a few minutes. If you have some pleasant meditation music, it is a good idea to use it because it can be a wonderful aid to relax your body and your mind for the focus exercise. In the meditation style you usually sit or recline in a relaxed position while you do your reading. Try both methods of focus and you will be able to discern which is best for you. You may also try different time-frames for your focus. Everyone's time-clock is different. If you're not a morning person, try doing your focus in the evening. It really doesn't matter when you focus or by what method, so long as the focus sessions are being done in a way that is effective for you.

NO TIME TO FOCUS
This is only an excuse. Always remember that where there is a will there is a way! If you want something badly enough you can always find a way to get the job done. If you don't…you won't! Here's a good story to punctuate this point. I once had a client who was having a bit of a challenge finding time to focus. At the time she was seven months pregnant and already had eight children to care for who ranged in ages from two to twelve years old, children whom she also home schooled! In addition to caring for her children, she was also responsible for the bookkeeping and paperwork for her husband's busy insurance business! Her days typically started at 5:00am and did not end until she'd finally collapse into bed around 11:00pm. Her question to

me was, "How can I possibly find the private time I need to focus?"
Well she had me there for a minute! It would definitely be a challenge,
but again, anything is possible if a person wants it badly enough.
Voila! After some deliberation I had an idea for her to try! If we laminated the focus cards for her to hang in the shower, she could focus
while she was taking her shower in the mornings! Well, that plan was
so successful that she also laminated another set for her kitchen so that
she could do her affirmations while she was cooking. This just goes to
show you, that if you want something badly enough, you can always
find a way!

STICKING TO THE PLAN
Not enough emphasis can be put on the importance of sticking with
the commitment to focus daily. Missing even one day can cause you to
lose valuable ground and break your new belief patterns that are form-
ing. If you only have minimum time, then focus to whatever degree
you can for that day. Even if it is nothing more than a quick glance
through your focus cards, it will be far better than doing nothing at all.
The optimum plan is for your daily focus exercises is for them to be
performed every morning, at this same time and in the same setting. If
mornings do not work best for you then pick a time that does work for
you and above all be consistent.

RESISTANCE IS TO BE EXPECTED
When you begin doing your daily focus exercises, it is normal for it to
feel extremely awkward in the beginning and you can expect to
encounter quite a bit of resistance from your conscious mind. This
stage is perfectly normal and will eventually pass if you continue to be
diligent with your daily efforts. With each affirmation spoken day by
day, you are breaking down the conscious mind's resistance a little bit
at a time. With great persistence on your part, your conscious mind's
resistance will eventually be overcome and you will start to see results
and actually start to enjoy the exercises. It is very important that you
know, that during the initial uncomfortable stage, even though your
conscious mind is resisting your new affirmations, you are still making
headway with the subconscious phase of your mind! The words you
are speaking are still slipping past the conscious mind and are getting
through to your non-judgmental subconscious mind. The message is
able to get through intact because your subconscious mind is com-

pletely non-judgmental and totally receptive every word that it hears in your own voice. It literally hears and blindly accepts every word you say without question. Through your diligent emotionalized repetitions the subconscious mind will ultimately be embedded or reprogrammed with the new input. Voila! Success! You are hereby reprogrammed and will see results! Once your new life characteristics are successfully embedded deep into your subconscious mind through this intensive repetition technique, they are automatically read and acted upon by God's creative mechanism. This is when your new lifeprint starts to become reality! How many affirmations will it take to embed the new input? That can vary. Typically, the less resistance you have to positive change in that particular area, the fewer affirmations it will take to embed. Whereas, the more resistance you have, the greater number of affirmations it will take. Of course, increasing the frequency of your focus sessions to several times a day can radically accelerate the process if you need results right now.

THE POWER OF THREE (OR MORE) REPETITIONS

When using your focus booklet, you will have several focus cards dedicated to the custom affirmations you will have chosen to represent your new lifeprint for every major category of your life. While doing your daily focus exercise, you will be repeating each one of the custom affirmations you selected three times, with as much passion and emotion as you can muster. Why is it important to repeat each one three times? Because the triple repetition of each affirmation will concentrate it with enough intensity for it to begin to wear down the resistance of your conscious mind and sink into your subconscious mind. Of course the more repetitions you use, the faster you are going to breakthrough the conscious mind's resistance and program the subconscious mind. So it may be a good idea during the first twenty-one days of your programming, for you to use more than three repetitions of each affirmation to facilitate a more expedient breakthrough of the barrier of your conscious mind, if you want results right away.

VISUALIZATION

When you have successfully broken through your conscious mind and are reaching the subconscious level, it is natural for wonderful images of yourself living your new life, to start springing into your imagination while you are saying your affirmations. When this happens it is a very good sign! It is a signal that you are starting to crystallize your new lifeprint deep within your subconscious mind. When these images come into your imagination, stop and take the time to enhance, embrace and love them. Walk through your images loving them, touching them and connecting with them in your minds eye. The Bible says, "That if two of you agree on touching any thing that they should ask, it shall be done." (Matthew 18:19) There is power in the sensation of touch, and it plays a far more important role in the creative process than was previously known. The most effective style of imagery is one where you take your time. Slowly walk through your mental scene step-by-step in real time, as if you were actually there having the experience. Physically connect with everything around you in your scene, fully incorporating all your senses; touching the sumptuous fabrics, feeling the smooth granite countertops, enjoying the warm embrace of your beloved, smelling the aromatic spring flowers, feeling the warm ocean breeze, hearing the crickets on a warm summers evening, and tasting the fresh squeezed orange juice and loving everything you are seeing, feeling and touching.

To help to further anchor your wonderful new images, you can look through various magazines and find pictures that best represent your mental scenes and cut them out and paste them to the backs of your focus cards (feel free to add extra pages for your images as needed).

Remember that it is the love that is your conduit to real creative power, but, it is your physical sensations of touch, taste, smell and sound that build the bridge necessary for the images you are holding in the invisible to cross over into the visible realm.

Follow these instructions very carefully and spend as much quality time as you can on your imagery exercises because it is the highest form of programming there is and it will radically accelerate your results. Cues to remind you to do your imagery exercises are at the bottom of each of your focus cards.

JUMP START

For optimal results you may want to do your daily focus exercise more than once a day for the first twenty-one days of your new program. The beginning of your focus program is the most difficult phase, because it is during this phase that your conscious mind offers the most resistance to your new programming. You already know that it takes frequent emotionalized repetitions of each of your affirmations for them to breakthrough your conscious mind and to be embedded into your subconscious mind, and this knowledge literally gives you the ability to decide how long it will take for this process to start working in your life! If you want immediate results, then start walking in alignment and do your repetitions as often as you can. With the frequent performance of your daily focus exercise, common sense tells you that results are going to occur much faster than they would with only one focus session per day. So you're in the driver's seat, how fast do you want to go?

USE A CALENDAR

Use a calendar to chart your daily focus exercises. Put a calendar up somewhere where you can see it, mark your start date for a "twenty-one day challenge" and decide in advance what your daily focus program will be for that twenty-one day period and beyond. At the end of each day, if you kept your focus commitment give yourself a star! If you didn't, that's alright just try to do better the next day. Strive to get a perfect twenty-one day score and you will be well on your way to a disciplined daily focus and your new life! Remember, that this exercise is to help you to create a lifetime daily focus habit, not a short term one.

MOMENTUM

When you start to get results, doubt will naturally start to be dispelled and you'll begin to feel a greater sense of confidence and excitement in the process. With tangible results beginning to occur, you will naturally begin to become more and more excited about the miracles that are happening! The excitement feeds the process and causes a wonderful snowball effect. In this stage you are lined up to enter into the optimum momentum phase or what I call the quantum leap effect (only available if you are walking in alignment). The quantum leap effect is the stage of maximum acceleration. A serious precautionary note for you here; for some unknown reason, as already mentioned, at this stage many people feel like it's alright for them to back off their daily focus sessions and coast on wonderful momentum they have already created. This is an enormous mistake. You must keep your good flowing, by remaining consistent with your daily regimen! Missing even one day of focus can cause you to lose the momentum you worked so hard to create. And believe me the last thing you want to do at this stage is to lose momentum and have to go back to square one to create your momentum again.

SUPPORT GROUPS

It is a very good idea for you to form your own support group. Application of these steps can be greatly improved by the accountability and support that a group can offer. It doesn't have to be a large group. It could just be you and a buddy. During the most resistant phase, which is usually your first twenty-one days, you and your buddy/group may want to talk or e-mail each other for support daily and then talk or meet weekly thereafter for as long as it is beneficial. During your phone calls, e-mail or meetings you can go over your rating sheets, rating your application of the seven steps for the week (the rating sheet is provided at the back of your book for you to do this and is titled "Daily Commitments."). Then, after everyone has rated themselves, you can discuss ideas to help those who have low ratings improve the areas where they are having challenges. You can also put a prayer bowl out (if you are meeting in person) for everyone to drop their confidential prayer request into and at the end of the meeting everyone in your group can decree all the prayers in the bowl answered. Make sure that every one in the group is in proper alignment and then repeat the following statement in unison, "We all agree that all the prayer requests in this bowl are hereby answered, by divine decree we all agree that it is hereby done. Thank you God!" A decree offered by two or more people who are walking in alignment will cause incredible miracles and breakthroughs to happen for those in your group who are in need of them! You can also share your miracle stories with each other to keep each other motivated! A support group can be a lot of fun and can play an important role in your committed application of the process. Don't wait for someone else to take the initiative to form a group, form your own! When you do, be sure that you send an e-mail to kayhaugen@sbcglobal.net to register your group, with the name and contact number of your group leader, your city and the number of members in your group, and you may get a personal visit from me to your group! Special note: It would be far better for you to embark on this journey alone than to team up with people who are not truly committed to following the program. So just be sure that the people you chose for your group are as committed as you are. If you start your group and find that those who were initially committed lose interest or drop out, don't let that stop you! You keep going, no matter what!

BREAKDOWN OF FOCUS EXERCISE

Every word you speak in the context of your focus exercises has a profound and important impact on the outcome you will experience with this program. The words in this program have been very carefully selected and the meaning of each word is designed to have a specific desired effect. Here is a more complete breakdown of the words and phrases that are contained in your focus booklet in the back of your book.

My New Lifeprint
(Title page of your focus booklet)

Purification
With God's help, I now completely forgive everyone for every erroneous, thought, deed and action they have ever committed toward themselves, others and God and forgive myself for the same. I now request the forgiveness promised to me by my Heavenly Father and accept the purification and renewal of my soul that comes through His forgiveness and now commit my life to only a life of good.

Unconditional Love and Charity
I now release unconditional love into the world. It flows forth freely from my heart blanketing the world with comfort, love, peace and the blessing that every need will be answered now with overflowing abundance. I now help others who are less fortunate than I whenever I can and to whatever extent I can. Freely I give good into the world and freely good comes back to me many times over.

Entering the Miracle Realm
With God's help, I now walk each and every day in perfect obedience and as I do, I rise above the everyday limitations of this world and enter into God's supernatural realm of miraculous possibilities that exists right here, right now.

Breaking Through to a New Life
With God's help my current and past reality no longer determines how far I can go. I now breakthrough and soar above my current levels of health, love, wealth, success and happiness, releasing all my past negative patterns that have prevented me from becoming all that I can be. I am now free to be anything I decide to be that is good for me and others. I now claim a new lifeprint starting this very moment and accept it as already being true for me *now* in the invisible realm regardless of my present appearances.

Set of Blank Cards
Blank cards for the eight major categories of your life for you to list the custom affirmations you have chosen for your new lifeprint: personality/spiritual, physical, friends, family, mate, financial, career and material.

Attainment Affirmation

As I walk in perfect alignment (unconditional love, forgiveness, obedience, faith and charity), the new lifeprint I have hereby chosen and have now accepted as my new life in the invisible realm, now becomes reality in my physical realm, in every perfect detail in accordance with God's unfailing law, in only the most expedient, harmonious, peaceful, perfect and beneficial ways possible for me and others in accordance with Heavenly Father's divine will.

I Go Forth With Gratitude and Expectation

I go forth this day in overflowing gratitude for all the good that is now happening in my life, repeating my attainment affirmation frequently and expecting my miracles to happen today and everyday.

My New Lifeprint

Purification

With God's help, I now completely forgive everyone for every shortcoming, imperfection and wrongdoing, they have ever committed toward themselves, others, God and me and forgive myself for the same. I now request the forgiveness promised to me by my Heavenly Father and accept the purification and renewal of my soul that comes through His forgiveness and now commit my life to only a life of good.

Unconditional Love and Charity

I now release unconditional love and a peaceful, non-judgemental acceptance of others into the world. It flows forth freely from my heart blanketing the world with comfort, love, peace, acceptance and the blessing that every need will be answered now with overflowing abundance. I now help others who are less fortunate than I whenever I can and to whatever extent I can. Freely I give good into the world and freely good comes back to me many times over.

Entering the Miracle Realm

With God's help, I now walk each and every day in perfect obedience and as I do, I rise above the everyday limitations of this world and enter into God's supernatural realm of miraculous possibilities that exists right here, right now.

Breaking Through to a New Life

With God's help my current and past reality no longer determines how far I can go. I now breakthrough and soar above my current levels of health, love, wealth, success and happiness, releasing all my past negative patterns that have prevented me from becoming all that I can be. I am now free to be anything I decide to be that is good for me and others. I now claim a new lifeprint starting this very moment and accept it as already being true for me now in the invisible realm regardless of my present appearances.

PERSONALITY/SPIRITUAL

PHYSICAL

FRIENDS

FAMILY

MATE

FINANCIAL

CAREER

MATERIAL

Blank Cards

Blank cards for the eight major categories of your life for you to list the affirmations you have chosen for your new lifeprint: personality/spiritual, physical, friends, family, mate, financial, career and material.

Attainment Affirmation

As I walk in perfect alignment (unconditional love, forgiveness, obedience, faith and charity), the new lifeprint I have hereby chosen and have now accepted as my new life in the invisible realm, now becomes my reality in the physical realm, in every perfect detail in accordance with God's unfailing law, in only the most expedient, harmonious, peaceful, perfect and beneficial ways possible for me and others in accordance with Heavenly Father's divine will.

⌒⌒

SUSTAINED BELIEF IN ATTAINMENT

Once the lifeprint for your new life has been clearly identified and successfully embedded into your subconscious mind, it is time to create and sustain the faith portal needed for your new life to be brought forth into reality. To accomplish this you must attain and sustain the pure, undoubting belief that your new life is coming forth *now* or in the present, moment by moment. This belief must be constantly sustained to maintain the integrity of the miracle portal long enough for your goals to have time to become reality. This can be accomplished through the use of an affirmation, called "The Attainment Affirmation."

WRONG WAY

New Lifeprint	+	Intermittent or No Belief in Attainment	=	Dreamer, No Results

If you have a clear new lifeprint of your desire firmly imbedded in your mind, but do not sustain the integrity of the miracle portal with the belief in the attainment of those goals or images, then you will only be a dreamer and will reap no results.

RIGHT WAY

New Lifeprint	+	Sustained Belief in Attainment	=	Success

REAL TIME

When you truly believe something is happening in the present moment, you open the portal for it to actually happen in the present moment. When you believe that your goals are coming to fruition in the present, this causes the most immediate path to those goals to be laid out before you in a highly accelerated fashion. Sustaining the belief that your new lifeprint is coming forth now in the very best ways possible, which is achieved through the use of affirmations, holds that perfect accelerated path in place long enough for your beliefs to become reality. It is like creating a miracle portal for your new life to become a reality. The primary goal in this step is to open the portal and to sustain it until your new lifeprint has time to come to pass.

"No problem can stand the assault of sustained thinking."
Voltaire

EXPECT SUPERNATURAL RESULTS NOW

To utilize God's creative force at its maximum level of possibility, it is necessary for you to be in alignment and to keep expecting your new life to materialize right now in extraordinary ways that go beyond the everyday. As you already know, God's creative force has the capacity to work in the supernatural while you are walking in perfect alignment. But your belief has to also be operating in the realm of the extraordinary as well in order for that to occur. By walking in alignment and expecting your new life to just effortlessly appear in the best ways possible, you create the optimum mental atmosphere for God's power to create the extraordinary circumstances needed to bring your goals to pass, in ways that will defy all logical explanation. In the optimum mental state you can enter into what I call the "the miracle zone." The miracle zone is a zone where the other laws of nature are actually superceded or overridden, allowing for such results as, spontaneous healings, the alteration of time and the physical elements and other incredible phenomena that defy explanation. This level of possibility may seem like an unattainable goal to you at this time, but as you begin to advance in your spiritual growth it will not seem as unrealistic to you at all, but perfectly natural. In short, if you want miraculous results, then don't hold realistic expectations. Realistic expectations restrict God's power from operating in the supernatural, because by law it is limited to operate within the "realistic" belief parameters that you have set forth. There are no limits to God's infinite potential except the limits you place upon it. Release the limitations by relaxing and expecting the extraordinary and stand-by for your supernatural miracles!

THE ATTAINMENT AFFIRMATION
The specific words used in the attainment affirmation are directives to God's creative power. The most beneficial means of directing your belief for the best possible outcome is covered in this affirmation:

> *As I walk in perfect alignment (unconditional love, forgiveness, obedience, faith and charity), the new lifeprint I have hereby chosen and have now accepted as my new life in the invisible realm, now becomes a reality in*
> *my physical realm, in every perfect detail in accordance with God's unfailing law, in only the most expedient, harmonious, peaceful, perfect and beneficial ways possible for me and others in accordance with Heavenly Father's divine will.*

AUTHORITY
Speaking the words of your attainment affirmation with authority, belief and conviction is very important if you want it to be effective. According to this scripture, "Thou shall also decree [to order or command] a thing, and it shall be established unto thee: and the light shall shine upon thy ways." (Job 22:27-28) God wants you to exercise the divine authority he gave you when you are walking in alignment. If you look up the word decree it means: an order or command issued by a person in authority. You are the captain of your own ship. If you ever forget you're in charge, then use one or more of these take charge affirmations to remind you of the truth;

> *"I am a child of God and by divine inheritance I have authority and dominion over my world and my circumstances."*

> *"I rule my circumstances—they do not rule me."*

> *"I am in charge of my thoughts and beliefs and therefore I am in charge of my life!"*

THE DIFFERENCE BETWEEN HOPING AND KNOWING

By relentlessly repeating your attainment affirmation, you can break-through the outer shell of doubt and limitation within your conscious mind, and attain a level of pure unquestioned belief or *knowing*. This is the level of belief for results and is a level well beyond hoping. There is an enormous difference between the two, and here is the difference…one works and the other doesn't. Trying to tell yourself that you believe, when you really don't, is futile! How can you tell? You'll know when you have entered into the *knowing* state, because there's no mistaking it—you know that you know and there is no doubt. You are certain! Many have told me, that while they were in this state of knowing, they've been overcome with euphoric feelings of joy and they could actually feel the miraculous power of God working within them. I too, have had these feelings, frequently to the point of crying tears of joy. You will know when you have touched the power of God. There truly is a *miracle zone*, and when you enter it, there's no question that you're there.

THE POWER OF REPETITION…THE SECRET TO YOUR NEW LIFE.

Anyone can attain this level of belief, if they want to badly enough. It's only a matter of breaking through the barrier of resistance that exists within your conscious mind and everyone is capable of doing it. Think of this resistance, like a hard outer shell you're going to have to chip through. Until this shell of resistance is broken through you are not effectively reprogramming. Breaking through this shell of resistance is a *mandatory* part of this process, because it is only the pure belief in the attainment of your goals filtered deeply down into your subconscious mind that will begin to set the wheels of creation in motion. God's infinite creative power within you only hears and acts on words that are wrapped in pure belief. You can't fool it! How do you chip through? With every authoritative, emotionalized repetition of your attainment affirmation you are chipping away at the resistance of your conscious mind. By using the *power of ceaseless repetition*, you can wear down the resistance in your conscious mind, breaking through the resistance barrier. The conscious mind cannot resist a *constant barrage* of affirmations; it eventually breaks down and begins to accept what is being said as true. Once this affirmation has successfully broken through the resistance of the conscious mind, you will start to really believe, and once you do, that belief will be acted upon by God's infinite creative power and you will start seeing results! Once you have achieved this break-through then you will want to actively sustain this state of belief until your new lifeprint has time come to pass. This can be accomplished by frequently repeating your attainment affirmation throughout the day, which can be done while you are performing ordinary tasks such as; driving, cleaning, cooking, exercising, grocery shopping, gassing up the car, walking the dog, taking a shower, shaving, etc. These frequent repetitions will successfully sustain the belief and keep the miracle portal open. It may take great discipline to accomplish this, but believe me your new life will be well worth it!

CONDENSING YOUR ATTAINMENT AFFIRMATION INTO A FAITH MANTRA

A new shorter version of your attainment affirmation can be anchored to have the same meaning of the full version. This can be beneficial to you because a shorter version will be easier to remember and repeat frequently throughout the day. It could be as simple as this, "My new life comes forth now." To anchor this affirmation (or one that you cre-ate in your own words), speak your full attainment affirmation once and the follow it with this mantra for a couple of minutes or so. Do this again and again throughout the day for several days and eventual-ly the shorter version will have the same meaning as the full affirma-tion to your subconscious mind.

THE PATH MAY BE STRANGE

As your new lifeprint begins to unfold, the path that is set forth for you to follow may seem odd or illogical to you. Be prepared, because the path you are put on may not always make sense to you according to your limited view. In fact, at times it may be so strange you may wonder how you could possibly be on course! This is why it is so criti-cal for you to maintain your belief with the consistent repetitions of your attainment affirmation, no matter what bizarre twists and turns your life may take along the way or whether you do or don't see results. Don't question! Just keep believing! During your journey no matter how strange, you must never stop believing for one moment that you are on the perfect course or you really will be thrown off course! (That sentence is so important that I want you to go back a read it again.) Don't allow slow results, strange results or the events you may perceive to be negative to rob you of your unwavering belief! With the limited awareness of your conscious mind, you cannot know the necessity of the things that are occurring in your life. If you truly believe, you can rest assured that the things that you may initially perceive to be negative, in hind sight, will turn out to be necessary steps in the process of the realization of your new life! They have to...because it's the law! So just relax, believe and faithfully continue to follow the steps laid out before you. In your attainment affirmation, you have asked for everything to happen in ways that will be a blessing to all concerned, which means that nothing that's is going to happen in the process of your new lifeprint being realized can be negative for you or anyone else. So, tell yourself that no matter what happens, that it's all happening for positive reasons, even if you have no idea what those reasons could possibly be. Events like the sudden loss of a job, an important appointment being rescheduled, a breakup, a flat tire or a red light when you are already late, may not be negative at all...but necessary, for reasons that may not be readily apparent to you with your limited view in the master plan for the perfect realization of your new lifeprint. These strange circumstances can throw you off course, only if they cause you to lose your faith and doubt. If you allow that to happen then you really will be off course!

THE OPTIMUM STATE

In the proper application of this step, the optimum state you will want to achieve is an intense, sustained, emotionalized, unwavering belief. You will want to work toward attaining a level of belief that is absolutely pure and then concentrate it into a continuous unbroken stream. Once you're in this "miracle zone" you will want to maintain this unbroken stream or miracle consciousness. Beginners may only be able to do for a short while before their thoughts begin to wander. But with practice, dedication, discipline and relentless affirmations you can learn to sustain this state of mind throughout the day. It may not always be in the forefront of your thinking but it will constantly be there in the back of your mind and that is the goal!

THE PURE BELIEF TEST

Here's a simple test to see if you have attained pure belief. Ask yourself these questions, "Am I the least bit worried about my future?" "Do I actually believe that my new life is going to happen?" What are your honest answers? If they are not what they should be, then you have more work to do with your attainment affirmation! Doubt, worry and fear are the opposites of faith and will rob you of your wonderful new life! In fact, worry and fear are more dangerous than that, because that they can bring the very thing you fear upon you. "The thing which I greatly feared is come upon me." (Job 3:25) Remember, whatever you think about both good and bad, you bring about! So, keep these dream-stealing, destructive thoughts out of your mind by following the instructions and repeating your attainment affirmation frequently throughout the day. With multiple repetitions, all worry, fear and doubt will begin to vanish. Like running clean water through a milky glass, the power of repetition will eventually prevail and you will eventually believe without any doubt!

MEMORIZE
You will want to memorize the attainment affirmation and repeat it or its condensed version throughout your day. If a doubt should enter your mind, remain calm and immediately repeat your attainment affirmation again and again. Do this until your belief has been successfully reinstated. The more time you spend believing that your new lifeprint is coming forth in perfect ways, the faster you will experience the life of your dreams.

Whenever you repeat or contemplate the attainment affirmation, you are redirecting and focusing God's infinite creative power to accomplish your new desired life. While you are focusing on your attainment affirmation, God's creative power is able to produce, create, coordinate and place in your immediate path whatever is necessary for your heart's desires to become reality. While you are focusing, you are actually creating the space for God's mighty power to redirect your fate toward the perfect creation of your new lifeprint. By performing your repetition exercises frequently, you are, in effect, maintaining the perfect path long enough for your wonderful new life to have time to become a reality. During your negative and non-focused periods, God's creative force has no other choice but to be redirected back through your old programming and you will be on course to get more of the same old

stuff. God's law is immutable, unfailing and unchangeable and is working 24 hours a day. If insufficient mental time is given to the attainment
of your new desires, your old patterns will continue to repeat indefi-
nitely according to the law.

During your conscious hours, you will want to strive to continuously
redirect God's creative force toward the task of realizing your new life
for you by using every available moment by repeating and contemplating your attainment affirmation. This takes true commitment and
discipline. You must be one-hundred percent committed to making the
full effort everyday, if you intend to live the life of your dreams. You
will know that you are performing this step correctly when you have
attained and are **consistently** maintaining the necessary state of pure
belief.

WATCH FOR SIGNPOSTS

Watch your life daily for any unusual happenings, coincidences or
strange occurrences. These are signposts to the achievement of your
desires! Observing these signposts will help increase your belief in the
process and help you move toward the optimum acceleration phase.
For example, if you want a new black Mercedes and you begin to
notice that you're attracting them with uncanny frequency, first be
aware that it's not happening by accident, and secondly know that it is
your focus that is attracting them to you. The forces of the law are
beginning to work on your partially formed programming. However,
because your programming has not fully crystallized into the firm conviction necessary for the full achievement of your goal, you have not
fully attained that goal for your own personal use, you have only
attracted it to you. For example, in the perfect relationship you are
seeking you could attract someone with so many of the attributes you
were looking for, that you're sure they have to be the one! When, in
reality they are only a signpost. Your programming for your ideal partner is starting to take hold, but because it has not been fully embedded
in your subconscious mind with multiple repetitions, this person
you've met turns out to be "close to what you are asking for—but no
cigar." If this should occur, the longer you hold on to the "mistake or
signpost," the more difficult it will be to let go and create the space for
the right person to come in. See all the signposts you experience as a
sign that your programming is taking hold, but that your program-

ming is not yet embedded strongly enough for you to fully realize that desired goal. It like a cake that's only half-baked or like Jell-O that hasn't quite jelled yet, you are going to have to keep going before you get the finished product. Keep doing your daily affirmations diligently and you will firmly crystallize your goals in your subconscious mind. Don't worry! It will work! Signposts can show up in a magazine, on television, in a café, on a billboard, as an idea, or in any other number of interesting ways. Just know that when they show up that they are by no means happening by accident, because there are no accidents. The signposts that begin to appear are your first evidence that the programming process is beginning to take hold and work! With this first proof, your belief and expectations become stronger and stronger. And the stronger your belief and expectations become, the more proof you'll get. The more proof you get, the more excited you become and the more results you will get. This natural effect is the snowball effect—a snowball effect of results that just gets bigger and faster until it finally builds into a level of momentum that is unstoppable.

RECORD KEEPING

To aid in the creation of this snow-ball effect, you will want to keep a record of all the unusual experiences that are happening in a success diary. Keep your diary handy because you will want to write things down as they happen, so that you don't forget. You can use a small tablet or your existing appointment book or whatever you prefer. This exercise can prove to be an important one because recognizing and documenting your intermediate successes will help to build your enthusiasm and strengthen your belief in the process.

GUARDING YOUR THOUGHTS

Do not shut down the fulfillment process by ever thinking or saying that "Nothing is happening!" or "This isn't working!" Because every thought you allow into your mind is being read and projected and these type thoughts will be picked-up and will sabotage you! You must carefully guard yourself against all negative thoughts regarding the process. The moment you think nothing is happening or that the process is not working—nothing *will* be happening and it won't be working because your negative thoughts just shut it down! Remember to be consistent with your belief no matter what. While performing this process, just remember that it is normal for you to see major break-throughs happening in some areas, with no visible progress in others. Remind yourself that this may be because it's not time in the sequence of things for those particular goals to happen yet and there is also the fact that many things are occurring behind the scenes, out of your limited range of view. If doubts start to arise, continue to remind yourself of these two facts so that you don't become discouraged and sabotage yourself when your good could be just around the next corner!

You can't fool God's non-judgmental power. It's listening to every word and following your instructions…garbage-in, garbage-out.

If you start telling yourself that things are happening either too fast, too slow or not at all—that's the outcome you'll experience. One way or another, God's non-judgmental power doesn't care. Everything you think or believe directly affects the rate of results and direction that your path takes. God's non-judgmental power doesn't care or know the difference. It does not judge…it only validates. Think everything is working and unfolding perfectly and dominate your mind with those thoughts and you will remain on a perfect and true course. Think you are off course and you will be off course until you decide to think you are back on course. This is why what you *allow* yourself to think moment by moment is very important!

WHATEVER IS NEEDED IS PROVIDED
So long as you continue to follow this step, along with all of the others, major action will be taking place in your life. Much of what will happen will be obvious to you, but as just mentioned, alot of what is taking place will be hidden from your view. While you are in the process of believing, behind the scenes all sorts of special arrangements are being made for your new life fall into place in the most perfect ways, order and time possible! Whatever is needed, at the precise moment it needs to unfold, is already pre-staged and is waiting ahead for you in your path and will remain there if you will keep the faith. Remember your job is to only keep believing and faithfully follow the path, not to judge the path. Like dominoes that are set up in a straight line, all the perfect events and arrangements needed for your new lifeprint to unfold are already pre-staged to happen and are ready to happen at

the precise moment that they should. You may not see any evidence whatsoever until it's time for those particular dominos to fall at the perfect time. Just align, program, believe and trust. Keep the faith and do not worry or be anxious about how or when things are going to happen and it will happen when you least expect it!

This step is not going to be what you would most likely expect preparation to be. The type of preparation that this step calls for, has nothing to do with planning the practical steps for the achievement of your goals. That would be outlining how your good is to come to pass and as you will recall, that severely restricts God's perfect creative process from operating as it should. Remember, in this process it is critical that you do not try to figure out the middle part between where you are and where you are going. The middle part is none of your business! Your job is simple, walk in alignment, program where you want to end up and then leave the *how* you are going to get there to God's perfect, all-knowing, limitless resource. Affirmations you can memorize and use if you have trouble with this part of the application process are:

"All my good is coming to me now in the most perfect and positive ways and how is none of my business!"

"I believe my new life is coming forth now in only the best ways. "How" is God's business, not mine!"

These affirmations or one you create on your own can be used whenever you get stuck in the thought process of figuring out the *how.* As you are already aware, outlining *how* shuts down your link to infinite possibilities and redirects your path through your limited conscious

> *"The secret of success in life is for a man to be ready for his opportunity when it comes."*
>
> Benjamin Disraeli

mind. Instead, you must simply trust in the ability of God's creative force to know what the perfect way is for you.

PREPARATION DEEPENS AND REINFORCES YOUR BELIEF

The correct form of preparation for this step will be the act of preparing in whatever safe ways you can to *receive* your new life. While you are preparing to receive, you are deepening and reinforcing your belief, which is vital for the process to work. Why does it deepen and reinforce your belief to prepare or get ready to receive your new life? Because when you get ready to receive something, you must really *believe* it is coming! For example, if you really believe that you are going to receive a new wardrobe, then wouldn't you go ahead and clean out your closet to make the space for your new clothes? If you were really certain that great wealth was coming to you, then wouldn't you begin to plan your investment portfolio now? Check interest rates? Select your bank and choose the charities you will be generously contributing to? If you have a goal to expand your company and you really believe that is going to happen, then you wouldn't you find your new location, pick out the furniture and make a list of the new positions you will need to fill? The act of preparation deepens your belief, because the act of preparation sends the message to your subconscious mind that you really believe these things are going to happen! To prepare in the correct manner, do absolutely everything you can now to safely and responsibly (it is not necessary to spend any money at this point) prepare to receive all aspects of your new life. If you want immediate results, then start preparing to receive your new life now. Do this exercise to the best of your ability, with as much detail as you can and you will start the snowball of results rolling!

PRIMING THE PUMP

By starting this preparation process now, you are "priming the pump" of the creative process. You are sending a signal to God's creative force that you not only believe, but have a belief that is strong enough to motivate you to take the positive actions needed to get ready to receive that good. The positive action of preparation causes a powerful reaction in the creative process, unleashing incredible forces that get the ball rolling toward your new life very quickly. So, get going and prepare!

MAKE A LIST OF WAYS YOU CAN PREPARE

Goals to prepare to receive	Ways to prepare to receive them
1. _____	_____
2. _____	_____
3. _____	_____
4. _____	_____
5. _____	_____
6. _____	_____
7. _____	_____
8. _____	_____
9. _____	_____
10. _____	_____
11. _____	_____
12. _____	_____
13. _____	_____
14. _____	_____
15. _____	_____
16. _____	_____
17. _____	_____
18. _____	_____
19. _____	_____
20. _____	_____

STEP SIX

GIVING

"The rich get richer and the poor get poorer." We've all heard that say-ing before and over time it has proven itself to be a true statement. Have you ever wondered why that is? Well, there is a reason why this tends to happen and it has to do with God's Law of Cause and Effect. Basically, as you will recall, this law says that whatever you think about…you bring about. Well, the rich naturally think thought trends of abundance,
so according to this unfailing law they will attract more abundance; financial windfalls, good fortune, record-breaking sales and so on. Conversely, poor people tend to think thoughts of lack, so they pro-duce more lack; drawing more and more debt and unexpected expens-es such as fender benders in the car, speeding tickets, dental expenses, illnesses that prevent them from working or they lose their jobs alto-gether. So, in simple conclusion, the rich get richer because they think about abundance and the poor get poorer because they think about lack.

BREAKING THE CYCLE OF LACK
The million dollar question is, "If we are suffering from lack and can't pay our bills, how do we stop worrying about money? Reality is star-ing us in the face…there is not enough!" Thoughts of lack are what we're naturally going to think about. So, how do we break this cycle? How do you hold thoughts of abundance when you don't have enough? The truth is that it is very hard to do and most people can't do it. This is where the Law of Reciprocation comes in. By utilizing this law, the cycle of lack can be broken.

THE LAW OF RECIPROCATION

What is the Law of Reciprocation? Basically it is the law that says that whatever you put out there into the universe (if you do so properly) is going to come back to you, *multiplied*. When you are already hurting financially it may seem unrealistic and impractical for you to give away money. So you think, I'll give away some of my time or some old clothes I don't need instead. Well, if you want to receive some free time or some old clothes back, then that's what you need to give away. But, if you want to receive money, then that is exactly what you need to give away.

THE IMPORTANCE OF CALCULATING THE PROPER AMOUNT

How do you know how much to give away? The rule of thumb to go by is to give what you can freely afford to give without ever worrying about missing it. More is not better! For emphasis let me repeat...more is not better! In fact, it would be far better for you to give less than you think you should in the beginning, than to give more than you should. This law is a delicate scale that if tipped in the wrong way can have the opposite effect. Giving away more than you can afford to give will backfire on you and keep you in the cycle of lack. So, start where you can now and as you prosper, you can work your way up to the standard accepted ten percent. But you don't have to stop there! You can always keep going if you are so inclined. It all depends on how much prospering you want to do. The successful application of this law, reminds me of a client I worked with several years ago. My client's name was Dorothy and her story was particularly sad. Because of an illness Dorothy had lost her steady job, had her car repossessed and could barely afford to eat and keep the lights on. Dorothy told me that she felt stuck and did not see how she could possibly afford to give any money away in her present situation. She was barely making ends meet with her babysitting jobs as it already was! I recommended that she start at whatever level she felt she safely could, even if that was only fifty cents a week. She thought about it and decided that if she gave up a few things, she could create some extra money to give. Hoping that the Law of Reciprocation would work, Dorothy made a commitment to contribute a dollar a week to the homeless, an amount she felt completely comfortable with. Sure enough her money began to increase, in the form of an extra babysitting job! When this happened she decided to raise her level of giving, up to three dollars a week just to see what would happen. And two more babysitting jobs came in! She upped the amount again to five dollars a week and out of the clear blue sky she was offered her old job back with a substantial raise! She had to take the bus to get there, but that didn't matter because she felt that through the use of the Law of Reciprocation, she was on her way back! She decided that with all of her good fortune she would raise her amount to ten dollars a week and shortly thereafter she was given a free car to drive! One of her co-workers learned that she didn't have a car and offered her one she wasn't using to drive at no charge! Slowly but surely Dorothy, through the Law of Reciprocation, was giving her way back to where she started. But when she got to where she started, she did not stop there! She kept on increasing the amount she gave week by week and kept on becoming more and more blessed financially. She was attracting more and more ways to prosper. Eventually, Dorothy was doing so well with her outside interests that she decided to quit her job altogether! Today, she owns her own successful company, drives a brand-new Mercedes, wears fine clothes, lives in a gorgeous home and gives away far more than ten-percent! Dorothy is now a firm believer in law of giving and wholeheartedly believes in the scripture, "Give, and it shall be given unto you; good measure, pressed down, and shaken together and running over shall men give unto your bosom." (Luke 6:38)

FEELING A SENSE OF CHARITY WHEN YOU GIVE
AND RECOMMENDED CHARITIES
"He that giveth unto the poor shall not lack: but he that hideth his eyes shall have many a curse." (Proverbs 28:27) In order for the Law of Reciprocity to work properly, it is imperative that you give, not out of a desire to recieve or out of fear, but from your heart, out of true charity. This is why it is important that you find a source to give to that really means something to you. When you find that right charity or charities or church and begin to give, take a moment each time you give to close your eyes and visualize your gift blessing the recipients (perhaps a child, a sick person, the hungry or the homeless) and see their appreciation. If you cannot think of a charity or church to give to, then you can donate to one of my favorites, The Salvation Army. They are a really good charity to contribute to because they contribute the

greatest percentage of monies they receive to the poor and as an added bonus they provide spiritual food in addition to the other goods and services they offer! The Salvation Army has a website for you to make online donations at www1.salvationarmy.org for your convenience.

But, my all-time favorite charity is **Life Outreach International**! This superb ministry reaches people all over the world who are in the most desperate need for hope, ministering, food, clothing, shelter, and good, clean water! There are many ministries out there, but few that are run with the integrity, generosity of spirit, righteousness and pure hearts that this one is! This is all very important, because if you give to a ministry that does not reach out and help the poor (as we were instructed by Jesus to do) with the same level of pure love that this one does, your tithes will come back to you *void*. If the ministry you give to is dead, your tithes will be dead. Life Outreach works folks! James and Betty Robinson, its founders, are the real deal. They are true, tireless, selfless servants of the Lord. The Robinson's, as good stewards of the money they receive in the name of the service of the Lord, do not pursue flamboyant lifestyles for themselves, not that it would be wrong for them to do more for themselves than they do I will tell you. They just choose to live modest lives and use the majority of the resources they receive for good works in the world, and this my friends, is what brings them *true* joy. The best way to contribute to this ministry is by way of the auto-draft. Start where you can and grow from there as your prosperity begins to increase, and it will! Contact information:

1-800-947-LIFE
Or go to www.lifetoday.org

MAKE A COMMITMENT TO GIVE AND BE CONSISTENT
Once you decide what the proper amount would be for you to start with, write it down on a piece of paper and make a firm commitment to follow through with your plan. Writing it down and making your commitment to follow through is very important. To firm up your commitment even further you can get on the auto-draft now or you can pre-write your checks for the next couple of months. Take your giving plan seriously and do not over-commit yourself with your plan or this exercise will

have the opposite effect, throwing you into more lack! To leave room for expansion, you can always say that this is where you plan to start now, but that as your prosperity increases, so will your generosity, even beyond 10-%!

YOU ARE ALREADY GIVING

If you have been giving consistently for some time and are not seeing an increase in your financial abundance, there can be five causes for this. One, you are giving to a dead charity or ministry. Two, you can afford to give more and aren't doing so—you have put a cap on your giving that is still under ten-percent, causing you to stagnate at the same financial level. The number three reason is not giving with a charitable heart. (Go back and reread this important segment if you are having trouble in this area.) Four, is that you are not willing to recieve. The number five reason is giving more than you should be giving at this point in time! Whatever the case, don't make big corrections, make small adjustments or you could overcompensate.

IT MAY TAKE TIME TO KICK-IN

When you initially start the giving process, it may take some time for The Law of Reciprocation to kick-in and start working for you. It is like pumping the handle on an old-timey water well pump. It usually takes several pumps of the handle for the water to start flowing, right? So, don't become disheartened if it takes a while. Be persistent with your commitment and once the flow begins, and it will because that is the law, it will increase as you increase your giving.

BLOCK OUT THOUGHTS OF LACK

In addition to using the Law of Reciprocation you will want to block out as many thoughts of lack as you can. Thoughts of lack will not stop the Law of Reciprocation from working, but they can really slow down the process. Whenever thoughts of lack enter your mind, block them out immediately by repeating, "Cancel, Cancel! NO EFFECT!" and repeat your attainment affirmation. It will also help you to remind yourself, that your current negative financial situation is only a temporary one and that your abundance is on the way! For example, if you see something you would like to have, don't say, "I could never afford that!" instead say, "I may not be able to afford that now, but I soon will!"

LIVING BELOW YOUR MEANS

Once you get on your feet and you are living the good life, in order to maintain it you will want to live below your means. Living above your means, no matter how rich you have become, will throw you into a lack consciousness and you will throw yourself back in trouble in no time. Remember the universal immutable Law of God that says *what you think about you bring about.* If you put yourself back into financial lack you will think thoughts of lack and cause your good life to be eroded away with one setback and unnecessary expense after another.

OVERSPENDING

Overspending is one of the worst forms of rebellion. It is pure evil! It is born of a desire to have things before you can afford to have them and people who make a habit of doing this never become wealthy! It is far better for you to be patient and wait until you can afford to buy something versus charging it and putting yourself into debt. Nothing will keep you in lack and financial desperation more than overspending will. If you are presently overspending or living above your means, then don't feel too bad because you are in good company. It is happening all across the country right now in epidemic proportions! Now, more than ever in history, people are demanding to have what they want now even though they cannot make ends meet as it is, making it a real challenge for all of us to keep up with the Joneses. This way of life has become a vicious cycle based on some sort of unspoken competition for us to out do one another. If you have gotten caught up in this vicious cycle, you should stop immediately, swallow your pride and do whatever you can to cut back now. Don't wait for the situation to escalate into desperate circumstances, take drastic measures now! You will be glad that you did, because it is going to take the pressure off you and put you on the fast track to prosperity. And remember that this cut back is only going to be temporary, because soon you are going to be prospering and able to afford anything you want and it will be within your means! Do the right thing now and you will end up being a real winner in the end, prospering abundantly without a worry in the world!

CHEATERS DON'T WIN

The quickest way to sabotage yourself from prospering is to take what doesn't belong to you, to cheat anyone out of what they are due or to take advantage of others. The Law of Reciprocation doesn't care—it will work just as effectively in reverse causing you to lose far more than you ever gained and will shut down the flow of good to you. The Law of Reciprocation works both ways…give and it will be given unto you in abundance—take and it will be taken from you in abundance!

DO NOT WISH ANY ILL UPON OTHERS

You don't want to wish ill on another person. The number one reason is because it is wrong. But, you also want to be aware that if anything actually happens to them as a result of your negative wishes or actions, it will come back on you. What goes around comes around! Leave them to pay for their own misdeeds through the Law of Reciprocation, and if they were truly in the wrong, nature will take care to see that they get their just desserts and then some! Barring being able to wish ill upon others, which you cannot do, you *can* pray for them to be bound from doing any more harm to you or anyone else and you can ask that any damage that they have caused you to be reversed! Here is a story for you…A very close friend of mine was violently attacked and raped while jogging late one evening by a stranger. Being keenly aware of the Law of Reciprocation, she prayed for her assailant to be bound from ever hurting her or others ever again and was very careful not to wish any ill will upon him. Only days later, this man was captured and sentenced to jail for thirty years for his crime against her as well as well as other crimes he had committed. As a side note: My friend later confessed to me that she had always harbored a secret fear of being raped. Unfortunately, the thing she feared had come upon her. Let this be a reminder to us to pray for protection for ourselves and our loved ones, and to banish all our secret fears with faith.

BE WILLING TO RECEIVE

Don't shut down the Law of Reciprocation by being unwilling to receive! You don't want to turn away your blessings when they show up. If you get in the habit of turning your blessings away, they will eventually give up and stop showing up! Many people who are selfless givers shut down the Law of Reciprocation because they don't know how to receive. Whenever someone tries to give something to this type

of person, it is always rejected. They say, "That's alright, I can manage." or "I appreciate your offer but I don't need your help." This pattern can be broken by gratefully accepting whatever comes your way.
It may also help for you to realize that by rejecting the kindness and
generosity of others, you are robbing them of the blessing they would
get back through the Law of Reciprocation. Here are a couple of affirmations to use to overcome this problem…

"In the past I used to experience an inability to freely receive,
but that is no longer true for me!"

"I used to rob others of their blessings by not accepting their generosity,
but that is no longer true for me, I now graciously accept their kind
offers and let them know how much they are appreciated!"

As a side note: Selfless givers tend to attract selfish takers because they
are the perfect complement to one another. The giver can bring these
imbalanced relationships back into balance by letting the takers know
that they expect them to reciprocate! Don't ever expect the takers to
recognize that things are horribly out of balance and to do anything
about it on their own, because that will never happen! It is one-hundred percent your responsibility to keep your relationships in balance.
If the takers refuse to reciprocate appropriately—then get yourself
some new friends!

STEP SEVEN

BE ONE HUNDRED PERCENT WILLING

With proper application of the other six steps in this process, God's creative power will have already aligned the perfect path for your new life to come forth. In other words, the dominoes are already lined up and are ready to fall in their perfect order.

Step number seven is designed to keep you on the right path for all the needed circumstances to fall into place at the precise time that they should. To do this step, you must be one-hundred percent willing to follow through with the things that are presented for you to do, with no hesitation. This step assures you that you will always be in the right place at the right time. As they say, "Timing is everything!"

A WILLING ATTITUDE KEEPS YOU ON COURSE

You have to be one-hundred percent willing to follow whatever path is presented for you to follow. The path can be presented in many ways. It can show up in the form of ideas, notions, hunches, guidance, intuitions and a host of other ways. Your willingness to act on the path being presented will keep your perfect timing on course, assuring you that you will be in the right place at the right time for your new life to fall into place perfectly. It is possible and not uncommon with the right attitude for your new life's goals to happen very quickly. If you are fortunate enough for that to happen, then not much will be needed in the way of actual effort for their attainment on your part. If it does not happen right away however, in order to assure that you remain on course, you

> "Nothing is impossible to a willing heart."
> John Heywood

need to be one-hundred percent willing to act without hesitation on whatever your conscience guides you to do. And not only must you be totally willing to follow whatever steps are presented for you to do, you must also perform the tasks presented with an extra effort toward neatness and perfection. The additional attention to neatness and perfection in performing these tasks is important even when no one else is ever going to see it. The reason? This extra attention to detail has a direct effect on the perfection of your divine alignment.

YOU REAP WHAT YOU SOW

An immutable universal truth is that you reap what you sow. The same measure of perfection and non-resistance you put out in your day to day efforts, is exactly what you are going to get back from God's creative process...amplified. This opens the door for your new life to come forth perfectly without hesitation, "right now." But, when you procrastinate and do things half-way then God's creative process will procrastinate and produce imperfect results! It is how the law works! Consistent follow through is critical for you to stay on the most immediate course possible. The proper timing and alignment for your new life to unfold can be seriously delayed without the proper application of this step. The steps you may be guided to take (cleaning out the garage, sorting and filing papers or taking a walk) may not seem to be directly linked to the achievement of your new life, but doing them is nonetheless essential to maintaining the perfect timing of the process.

LET YOUR TRUE CONSCIENCE BE YOUR GUIDE

Let your conscience be your guide, be careful not to let your own imagination misguide you into taking the wrong direction or overdoing it. A good way to know the difference between your own imagination and your conscience, would be that your true conscience would never put you in situations that would ever be unsafe, illegal, immoral, could potentially harm you, hurt others or overstress you. For example; you would never be guided to mow the lawn on the hottest day of the year in the middle of the day or to take a jog in a dangerous neighborhood late at night.

YOU WILL KNOW

When action from you is called for, it is usually presented to you in a very apparent fashion and you'll just know. I remember a specific instance back in 1984 when I was first utilizing this process. It was around 9:00 pm and I was already dog tired and in bed with the lights out, when that inner voice said, "You should get up right now; empty out all of your packed boxes, sort out the things you need to give away and put them in boxes for Goodwill ready to be picked-up tomorrow." I had a momentary reluctance to follow that guidance, and attempted to convince myself that it would be alright if I got up and did this first thing in the morning. Then, I remembered the importance of my commitment to be one-hundred percent willing to follow through on what my conscience guided me to do *without any hesitation*. Realizing that this step was necessary for me to be in the right place at the right time for the miracles I needed to show up, I was motivated to get up and get going right then! Well, the payoff that came from the obedience to my conscience that night was certainly well worth it to me in hind sight! Later that same night one of my neighbors, whom I had never met, knocked on my door at around 11:00 pm and handed me a job ad that she had clipped out of the newspaper. She said she had heard of my desperate situation and told me that she had been mysteriously compelled to bring me the job ad. Well that job later turned out to be the perfect job for me! In addition to that, it also turned out to be an important stepping stone in the accomplishment of several of my other goals. Later, as I reflected back on what had happened that night, I wondered if that neighbor would have been willing to knock on my door that late at night if my lights had been out and I really don't think so. My willingness to obey my conscience had without doubt put me in the right place at the right time!

In many cases where this step has been adhered to with absolute discipline, things have just seemed to fall out of the sky. Without the proper application of this step, your goals will still eventually come to pass, but they will take longer and will occur in more typical ways that will involve more work on your part. In order for this process to work in the supernatural realm, you must adapt the rock solid attitude that "I am willing to do whatever it takes without hesitation." Procrastination is your enemy number one. Don't let it prevent you from attaining the miracles that are waiting just ahead for you!

WHAT IS YOUR CONSCIENCE?

In order to be able to follow your conscience, you need to know what your conscience is. Your conscience is nature's built-in guidance system. The part of you that tells you what is right and is always gently urging you to do the right things.

Looking back over your life, what percentage of the time would you say that you have actually listened to your conscience and done the right thing? Twenty-percent? Fifty-percent? Eighty-percent? If you rated yourself at the twenty-percent level, then that would mean that you are living in rebellion to your conscience eighty-percent of the time! Rebellion is the act of ignoring your conscience and doing whatever it is that you want to do. Rebellion, unfortunately, can become as much of a habit as anything else in life. Rebellion is the true root cause for all bad behavior; smoking, overeating, staying out too late, sleeping in too late, drinking too much, stealing, committing adultery, eating the wrong foods, not exercising, refusing to clean up after yourself, overspending, etc. A life that is lived in rebellion always leads you down the road to misery, sickness, lack, destruction, divorce and unhappiness. Whereas a life lived following your conscience or living "righteously" leads you down the road to health, prosperity, success, love and happiness.

Basically, your conscience is your internal guidance for righteous living. The Bible says that nothing shall be withheld from him who walks in righteousness, which implies that if you are not living in alignment with your conscience or "righteously," your good will be withheld, or at least delayed and results have proven this to be absolutely true.

If you have made a positive habit of listening to your conscience and are already living in a state of righteousness; this step will be effortless for you. You'll just keep on doing what you've been doing.

BREAKING FREE OF REBELLION

But for those rebellious souls who have not been living this way, this may be one of the most challenging steps of all. With some people rebellion has become such a way of life, that they've lost touch with their conscience. To get back in touch or to reconnect with that part of you, get in the habit of asking yourself this question throughout your day, "If I were doing the right thing right now, what would I be doing?" Listen for the response from your conscience and then jump up and do whatever that is to the best of your ability without hesitation, RIGHT THEN! Do this over a period of several days and you will successfully reconnect with your conscience.

KEEP A TO-DO LIST

Keep a "To-Do List." On this list, put down the things that you need to do and the tasks you've been putting off. Prioritize your list in order of the worst thing first. Facing the most dreaded task first will jumpstart the process and make all the other tasks a piece of cake. I know that this may be a challenging undertaking for you, but it will get your miracle process going. This list might include things like; grocery shopping, picking up the dry cleaning, washing the dishes, getting the oil changed in the car, organizing your office, cleaning out your closets, clearing out your junk piles, balancing your checkbook, organizing your garage, making a new resume, writing thank-you notes, sorting your tax papers, making important calls, working out, cleaning out your refrigerator and kitchen cabinets, garment alterations and mending, etc.. You may have already gotten some of these things accomplished in the housecleaning projects that you have started in step two, if so, good for you!

MAKING APPOINTMENTS TO FOLLOW THROUGH

Scheduling appointments for you to complete your to-do list (worst first) and sticking to those appointments can be extremely beneficial. Having a scheduled time to complete these tasks can create the commitment and needed time to follow through. When the appointed time has come, don't make any excuses, feel the dread and do it anyway! Tell yourself that achieving success on the fast track is well worth the effort. Who wants their success to take any longer than it has to? Check off the tasks on your list one by one as you accomplish them. Don't start the next project on your list until you have finished the one before it and only do one project at a time! As you progress through your to-do list will begin to feel a wonderful sense of accomplishment and empowerment.

GET A PARTNER

If you have trouble getting started on a difficult project on your to-do list, find a partner to support you and then trade off appointments with them to help them with a difficult project they're facing. If you start asking for a partner (perhaps someone in your support group?), you will probably have no trouble finding friends who have certain projects they dread doing just as much as you are dreading doing yours. Supporting each other is a win-win situation!

POSITIVE EFFORTS COUNT!

You don't have to finish everything on your list to start reaping the powerful benefits from your efforts. As long as you continue to take sincere, consistent, positive action toward the accomplishment of each one of your tasks, you'll put yourself on the right path to the "land of milk and honey where miracles just land in your lap." You may slip up from time to time but that is alright, it's the continued effort that counts. Don't give up! Your journey may be challenging, but putting yourself on the right path to receive miracles is worth it.

You alone must choose the path you take. If you have been living a life of rebellion I hope you will choose to make these positive changes because remaining in a life of rebellion will only lead to misery, sickness and destruction.

DYNAMITE

Maybe you're intuition is gently prodded you to seek new employment, go back to school, to let go of an unhealthy relationship, start a healthy diet or get an exercise program going. Moving willingly toward these intuitive directives is the recommended course of action for you to take. You don't have to jump in with both feet at first if you are not quite ready, you can take it as slow as you need to. Just do your level best to make an effort no matter how small. However, if you are just stubborn and refuse to take any positive action at all, this can cause a "log jam." In a log jam, a log gets stuck in the stream by your refusal to follow the directives and take positive action, the log/resistance blocks the free flow of the other logs, causing a back up. God's creative force has a directive that you have given it, to get the logs downstream (bring your new life forth). It analyzes the problem and provides the sometimes unpleasant, but necessary force needed to make the needed correction. And believe me the force that it may see as necessary, is not the desired effect you are looking for. You don't want to put yourself in a situation where you are forced to take action before you were ready to do so. A prime example of this would be the sudden break-up of an abusive relationship. If the relationship is not dissolved in loving, peaceful ways as your conscience guided you to do, when it should have been done, eventually the pressure will build and there will be a nasty blow-up that will force you to move on when you were not prepared. The same effect can occur in your finances. In the case of finances for example, your conscience told you to stop over-spending, but you didn't follow the guidance when it was given and just kept on overspending. Now, you have no lights and no way to pay your bills! If you do not follow your conscience when you receive the gentle guidance from within, something will always occur to force you into a correction. Believe me, it's much easier on your nervous system to take positive action on your own, willingly! Not to mention the added benefit of putting yourself in the proper alignment for miracles.

ATTENTION OVERLOADERS
You may have convinced yourself that you're being obedient to your conscience, when in reality you've overloaded yourself with a level of responsibility and/or outside activities that are throwing you and your family out of balance. This is a serious problem that needs to be addressed. To bring your life back into balance, you must unload some of your unnecessary responsibilities and/or outside activities right now. Distribute them or delegate them accordingly, and bring your life and family back into balance.

I CAN'T SAY NO!
Do you have problems saying no? It is probably because you don't know a good way to do it! It can be a tricky thing to do because you don't want to let anyone down or hurt their feelings, right? But in real-ity you end up letting them down anyway, because there was no way you could handle the job without being in two places at the same time! Here's a positive suggestion for you, the next time someone asks you to do something you don't have time for you can say, "I would love to

help you with that, but I am already overcommitted and the last thing I want to do is let you down, but please keep me in mind the next time."

MAKING GOOD CHOICES ALONG THE WAY

In the process of your new life coming forth into reality you will be making choices...choices that must be in alignment with your own morals and plain old-fashioned common sense. It is important not to take any action that would go against your morals, hurt anyone, or put you or your family in any kind of risk spiritually, emotionally, financially or physically.

If you fully apply and master each of the proven steps in this process, miracles will happen and wonders will never cease, just like it has happened for countless others. Remember, as in life, you're going to get out of this program what you put into it!

GOOD LUCK WITH THE SEVEN STEPS AND GOD BLESS

FINALLY...BE SURE TO GET YOUR TICKET TO THE AFTERLIFE

"Because strait is the gate and narrow is the way, which leadeth unto life, and few there be that find it." (Matthew 7:14) In order to be truly saved, or to get your ticket into Heaven you must specifically claim the death of Jesus in place of yours for your sins (why will be explained just ahead). Until you do this you are not truly saved. A simple statement of faith for you to use to claim this most crucial of all promises:

**Lord Jesus, I accept the fact that you died
in my place as payment for my sins.
Thank you Lord Jesus for your loving sacrifice.**

But why are the wages of sin death in the first place? "For the wages of sin are death." (Romans 6:23) Well, there are three types of laws that we live under, those given to us by our spiritual hierarchy, namely Jesus and our Heavenly Father, the laws dictated to us by nature and those put forth by our governments. The law that determined that "the wages of sin are death," comes to us from the most unforgiving, inflexible and merciless sources of our laws, nature. While the other two sources provide a certain degree of grace, with nature there is *no grace whatsoever*. This is where Jesus comes in. Only Jesus, who has attained perfect authority over the natural laws, has the authority to supercede them. This is *why* Jesus had the power and the authority to declare that his death would count for us, as the wages required for our sins, if we would only accept it as such!

Because nature's impersonal mission is to constantly seek to perfect, balance, heal and harmonize the world and everything in it. *Anything*, that goes against the flow of that mission must be cut off, in the same context, as a harmful virus being eliminated from the body by the natural immune system. Nature's immune system works globally. Plain and simple, when you rebel or "sin" against your conscience which is nature's guidance system to perfection and harmony with the world around you, you are going against the grain of nature and *you must be cut off.* By being cut off, I mean that you will die a second death, the spiritual death. This means that you will be cut off from eternal life.

But what of eternal torment in hell? The wages of sin, according to the Bible, are *death*. Those who die the second death, the spiritual death, shall be permanently set apart from the kingdom. Energy can never be lost, but it can be transformed; as is true in the case of a log being burned in a fire. When a log is placed into the fire, its energy is transformed from its present state, into its new form which is heat. It is still energy, but a new transmuted form of energy that is far different from its original state. Jesus, through His connection to infinite intelligence, had access to this higher knowledge and knew of this price we would have to pay for our sins and because of His great love for us He created a means whereby we would not perish if we would accept His death in place of our own. This is how He saved us.

The first death you experience is the physical death. When this occurs you go into a resting state, where you exist in a non-physical dream state in either "Paradise" or "Hades" (depending upon the overall light vs. dark state of your own personal consciousness) until the final judgment day comes at the end of the seven year tribulation period, at which time

"Heaven" (Heaven and Paradise are not the same) is to actually be established by Jesus here on Earth.

The seven year tribulation or "Armageddon," is the great purification of Earth from all sin. An event that will occur as prophesied and outlined in the book of Revelation. The tribulation will begin to unfold when the balance scales of nature reach a tipping point and sin/darkness begins to outweigh good/light in our world, which as previously mentioned goes against the grain of the immune system of nature and that of God. This tipping point (which Jesus, through His supernatural ability to see all the way into the future, ultimately knew was going to come to pass) will ring in a perilous time of purification with unimaginable disasters; worldwide devastating epidemics, floods, earthquakes and volcanic eruptions of epic proportions, great famine and pestilence. Beware! For this is a time we could be perilously close to, if you take into consideration the runaway decline in morality, the devastation of our rain forests, the giant hole in our ozone layer, and the fact that we have become so incredibly desensitized to it all. The Bible says to, "Watch ye therefore and pray always that ye may be accounted worthy to escape all these things that shall come to pass... (Luke 21:36) But how will we escape? Well the Bible also tells us that Jesus has prepared a place for us, "And if I go and prepare a place for you, I will come again, and receive you unto myself (the rapture); that where I am, there ye may be also." (John 14:3).

You may be wondering, why our all-powerful Heavenly Father doesn't just intervene and stop the natural purification process from occurring? He cannot do that, because without this self-preserving system in place, our planet would not survive. He cannot take away the same system that holds the world we live in together, purifies our polluted waters, rebuilds the forests after we burn them down, heals our bodies of illnesses and continuously cleanses the air we breathe or our world would not survive. But our Heavenly Father did not leave us without a way...

"For God so loved the world, that he gave his only begotten Son, that whosoever believeth in Him should not perish, but have everlasting life." (John 3:16)

When the final judgment day arrives after the tribulation time, if you have met these three important requirements clearly outlined in the scriptures, you will have the keys to gain access into heaven.

1. You have accepted the fact that Jesus died for your sins. "For by grace are ye saved through faith; and that not of yourselves: it is a gift of God." (Ephesians 2:9)

2. You have been born of water and baptized in the Holy Spirit, "Verily, verily I say unto thee, Except a man be born of water and of the spirit, he cannot enter into the kingdom of God." (John 3:5) and...

3. You have done your best to live in accordance with your Heavenly Father's will, by loving God, yourself, and your neighbor as yourself. "Not everyone that sayeth unto me (on judgment day), Lord, lord shall enter into the kingdom of heaven; but he that doeth the will of my Father which is in heaven." (Matthew 7:21)

The scriptures are unmistakably clear on these three requirements. But how can you be sure that you will gain entrance into heaven on judgment day? The scriptures in St. Matthew 25:31-46 spell it out a little more clearly for you (you might want to take a moment to get your Bible as a reference source).

These scriptures explain that on judgment day that Jesus will be judging everyone based on their works (not their sins) and separating His sheep, those who will be joining Him in the kingdom, from the goats, those who will not. As a very important point here, the purpose for Jesus judging your works is for Him to discern whether or not you are truly His brethren. If you've truly been baptized in the Holy Spirit that will most certainly be reflected in your works, actions, deeds, fruits and gifts of the spirit. Evidently, in the eyes of Jesus your actions speak louder than words!

Your works, not your sins will be examined on this day, because if you have properly accepted the death of Jesus Christ in place of your own, your sins have already been forgiven by grace and have been blotted out from the records of your life. But your works, the good deeds you performed through your fruits and gifts of the spirit, will remain as a testimony of who you were in Christ. Now, you cannot be saved by your works; they are only your testimony to Jesus of your baptism in the Spirit and how He will recognize you as His brethren on judgment day, which is very, very important!

Once again for emphasis, it is only by the acceptance of the death of Jesus for your sins, that you can truly be saved. But, the acceptance of His death is not the only requirement for entrance into the kingdom. According to the scriptures, Jesus must see evidence through your works that you are truly His brethren and have been baptized in the Holy Spirit or He will not give you admission into the kingdom. Many theologians do not teach this, even though it is scriptural, and have unfortunately lead many, many astray. Beware!

In Matthew 25:32, we are told that on judgment day He will divide the people into two groups, His sheep on his right hand and the goats on His left (for another scriptural reference on this judgment of our "works," go to Revelation 20:11-15).

His sheep are those, who through their works, exhibited loving, charitable, caring actions throughout their lives…loving acts of kindness that were born of the true baptism of the Spirit of Christ in their hearts and whose names are also found written in the book of life (those who have accepted Jesus' death for their death).

What kind of works identifies you as one of His sheep? Well, as described in Matthew 25: 35-40, while you were here did you help to feed the hungry? Did you help to cloth and house the homeless? Did you visit the sick? Did you visit those in prison? Did you have compassion for those less fortunate than you? This is what you do and naturally how you live if you truly have the heart of Christ! All others, who have not lived their lives in this kind, loving, giving, caring, selfless and charitable way (even though they may have professed themselves to be Christians) are referred to as the goats.

To those He does not recognize as His true brethren on judgment day He will say, "And then I will profess to them, I never knew you (I don't recognize myself in you): depart from me, ye that work iniquity." (St. Matthew 7:23) And they will say to Jesus, didn't I heal the sick and cast out demons in your name? But tragically, they failed to realize that using the name of Jesus and having the true baptism of the Holy Spirit of Jesus in your heart are two entirely different things.

When you have been truly baptized in the Holy Spirit it is reflected through your "works." The scriptures in 1 Corinthians 13:1-3 tell us that even though we speak in tongues and have the gifts of prophecy, knowledge, faith, etc., that if we have not charity, or the true evidence of the fruit of Christ's love and spirit in our hearts, we are nothing! 1 Corinthians 13:4-7 breaks down what the Apostle Paul meant by charity in this way, "Charity suffereth long, and is kind; charity envieth not;

charity vaunteth not itself, is not puffed up, doth not behave itself unseemly, seeketh not her own, is not easily provoked, thinketh no evil; rejoiceth not in iniquity, but rejoiceth in truth; beareth all things, believeth all things, hopeth all things, endureth all things." Charity is synonymous with Christ's love and His nature and is what we should all desire and pray to have most if we want to be one of His faithful sheep!

If you make it into Heaven, which in accordance with the scriptures is to be established right here on planet Earth by Jesus at the end of the tribulation, what will it be like? The Bible says that no man can even comprehend how wonderful it will be. Our world will be basically the same; grass, trees, lakes and sky. Yet, it will be far different than it is now. It will be transformed by Jesus into a magnificent, magical place of endless abundance, health, joy, peace, love and happiness. Our heavenly world will be infinitely more beautiful, clean, perfect, bright and abundant than it is now, with no pain, illness, loneliness, fear, death or lack of any kind. A place where everyone's every want or need will be instantaneously created and every dream will come true. In this world, you will be so happy that your heart will remain in a constant state of joyous euphoria. The feelings of unconditional love you will feel toward everyone will cause your spirit to soar with a degree of freedom you have never known. You will be so full of joy, appreciation and gratitude for your Heavenly Father and Jesus that your heart will barely be able to contain it. In Heaven, you will live happily ever after with all of your brothers and sisters for all eternity. "For, behold, I create new heavens and a *new Earth*: and the former shall not be remembered nor come into mind." (Isaiah 65:17)

But, is Heaven the same for everyone? The Bible implies that in Heaven there will be different levels of reward for us. "In my Father's house are many mansions…" (St. John 14:2) and "lay up for yourselves treasure in Heaven…" (St. Matthew 6:20) These scriptures could imply that by diligently striving to live righteous, generous, loving, charitable lives, could rate you with the keys to the very best resort accommodations that Heaven has to offer!

DAILY

COMMITMENT SHEET

The daily commitment sheet is an important tool that you can use on a daily basis to monitor your application of the *Seven Steps*. This sheet is designed to be removed, enlarged for easier reading, copied onto colored card stock and then laminated to hold up to daily use.

Read your daily commitment sheet every morning. Because it is laminated you can hang it in your shower, put it on your bathroom mirror, by the toilet or anywhere else you like. If you will connect the reading of your Daily Commitment Sheet to a morning activity (like brushing your teeth), you can read it while you are performing that activity. By doing this you can easily be reminded to do the exercise and develop the important habit of doing it everyday.

FOR SUPPORT GROUPS
The daily commitment sheet can be a useful tool for your support group. Only instead of rating daily performance, it can be used to rate the overall weekly performance of each of the steps by those in your group. To use the daily commitment sheet for your support group, make copies of it for the meeting and get everyone to rate their performance for their week/month. Then, help those with low ratings improve by getting the group to come up with ideas to help them with those areas they are finding challenging. Two heads are always better than one to find ways to overcome challenges. Those who are sincerely interested in applying this process will really appreciate the group's support! Of course, if someone doesn't really want to apply the

process, all the positive suggestions in the world are not going to help because they won't be applied.

DAILY COMMITMENTS
TO BE READ EVERY MORNING

REALIZING THE UNLIMITED POTENTIAL OF GOD'S POWER – Today I will accept the belief that anything is possible if I can believe, into the deepest recesses of my mind.

CLEARING THE WAY THROUGH PERFECT ALIGNMENT – Today, with God's help, I will do my best to walk in unconditional love, forgiveness, obedience, acceptance, charity and pure faith.

PROGRAMMING MY NEW LIFEPRINT DAILY – Today I will read my daily focus booklet and embed my new lifeprint deep into my subconscious mind and I will do this everyday to the best of my ability.

SUSTAINING MY BELIEF IN ATTAINMENT – Today I will repeat my attainment affirmation frequently throughout the day and consistently maintain the space for the supernatural attainment of my new lifeprint.

WATCHING FOR SIGNPOSTS AND DOCUMENTING THEM – Today I will watch out for unusual events and remarkable occurrences and document them in order to strengthen my belief in the wonderful process that is now taking place in my life.

PREPARING TO RECEIVE – Today if there is anything I can safely do to prepare to receive my good, I will do so (may not be a daily exercise).

GIVING FREELY – Today I will take a moment to imagine the blessings that my financial tithes are providing to others. I will follow my plan and give on a consistent basis (weekly or monthly), and as my finances increase, I will increase what I give.

BEING ONE-HUNDRED PERCENT WILLING – Today I will be one-hundred percent willing to follow the positive path that is provided to me, and will do so without any resistance or hesitation.

CREATING AND FOLLOWING A TO-DO-LIST EVERYDAY – Today I create a to-do list and then accomplish what I put on my list. (It is alright if you don't complete your list, it is only important that you do your best!)

GOING FORTH WITH GRATITUDE AND EXPECTATION – Today I go forth with overflowing gratitude and positive expectation, expecting miracles today and everyday.

RATE YOUR APPLICATION
On a scale of one to ten, ten being best, how am I doing so far with the application of each one of these steps?

COMMITMENT TO IMPROVE
Today I am committed to improve upon all those steps which need improvement.

DAILY FOCUS

BOOKLET KIT

INSTRUCTIONS

STEP ONE – Cut out the all of the focus booklet pages along the guide lines, keeping the pages in their proper order.

STEP TWO – Make copies of these pages on a heavy card stock, use a colored stock if you like and cut out your focus cards. **VERY IMPORTANT:** make several extra copies of the blank cards, so that you will have extras, in case you make mistakes, need more room, or want to change your goals later. If you don't have ready access to a copier, then you can make your own focus cards by writing out the statements on large index cards.

STEP THREE – Using a single hole punch, punch holes where indicated by the shaded circles on your focus cards and stack the cards in their proper order.

STEP FOUR – Bind your focus booklet, by threading either some twine, thin ribbon, twist ties or binder rings (sold at most office supply stores) through the holes and then tie them off, but not too tightly.

Special Note: Be sure to maintain a clean copy of your originals in a file folder for later use.

My New Lifeprint

Purification

With God's help, I now completely forgive everyone
for every shortcoming, imperfection and wrongdoing, they have ever committed toward themselves,
others, God and me and forgive myself for the same. I
now request the forgiveness promised to me by my
Heavenly Father and accept the purification and
renewal of my soul that comes through His
forgiveness and now commit my life to only a
life of good.

Unconditional Love and Charity

I now release unconditional love and a peaceful, non-judgemental acceptance of others into the world. It flows forth freely from my heart blanketing the world with comfort, love, peace, acceptance and the blessing that every need will be answered now with overflowing abundance. I now help others who are less fortunate than I whenever I can and to whatever extent I can. Freely I give good into the world and freely good comes back to me many times over.

2

Entering the Miracle Realm

With God's help, I now walk each and every day in perfect obedience and as I do, I rise above the everyday limitations of this world and enter into God's supernatural realm of miraculous possibilities that exists right here, right now.

3

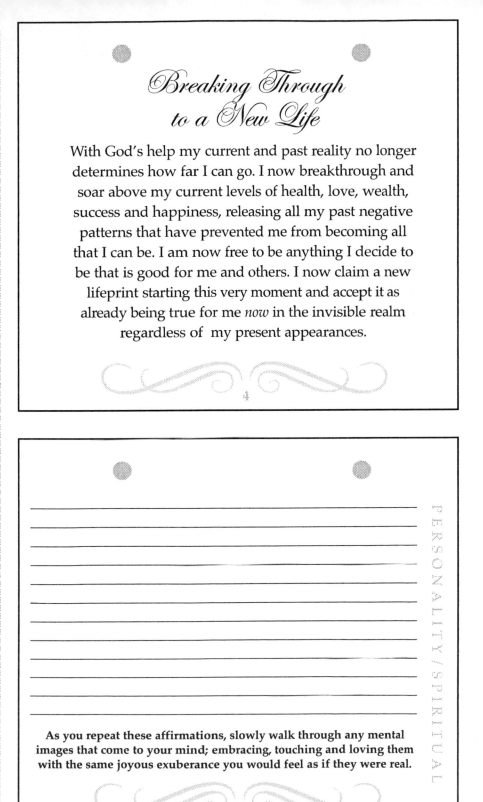

Breaking Through to a New Life

With God's help my current and past reality no longer determines how far I can go. I now breakthrough and soar above my current levels of health, love, wealth, success and happiness, releasing all my past negative patterns that have prevented me from becoming all that I can be. I am now free to be anything I decide to be that is good for me and others. I now claim a new lifeprint starting this very moment and accept it as already being true for me *now* in the invisible realm regardless of my present appearances.

As you repeat these affirmations, slowly walk through any mental images that come to your mind; embracing, touching and loving them with the same joyous exuberance you would feel as if they were real.

PERSONALITY/SPIRITUAL

PHYSICAL

As you repeat these affirmations, slowly walk through any mental images that come to your mind; embracing, touching and loving them with the same joyous exuberance you would feel as if they were real.

FRIENDS

As you repeat these affirmations, slowly walk through any mental images that come to your mind; embracing, touching and loving them with the same joyous exuberance you would feel as if they were real.

FAMILY

As you repeat these affirmations, slowly walk through any mental images that come to your mind; embracing, touching and loving them with the same joyous exuberance you would feel as if they were real.

8

MATE

As you repeat these affirmations, slowly walk through any mental images that come to your mind; embracing, touching and loving them with the same joyous exuberance you would feel as if they were real.

9

_____
_____
_____
_____
_____
_____
_____
_____
_____
_____
_____

As you repeat these affirmations, slowly walk through any mental images that come to your mind; embracing, touching and loving them with the same joyous exuberance you would feel as if they were real.

10

_____
_____
_____
_____
_____
_____
_____
_____
_____
_____
_____

As you repeat these affirmations, slowly walk through any mental images that come to your mind; embracing, touching and loving them with the same joyous exuberance you would feel as if they were real.

11

cut along dashed lines

MATERIAL

_____
_____
_____
_____
_____
_____
_____
_____
_____
_____
_____

As you repeat these affirmations, slowly walk through any mental images that come to your mind; embracing, touching and loving them with the same joyous exuberance you would feel as if they were real.

12

Attainment Affirmation

As I walk in perfect alignment (love, forgiveness, obedience, faith and charity), the new lifeprint I have hereby chosen and have now accepted as my new life in the invisible realm, now becomes a reality in my physical realm, in every perfect detail in accordance with God's unfailing law, in only the most expedient, harmonious, peaceful, perfect and beneficial ways possible for me and others in accordance with Heavenly Father's divine will.

13

I Go Forth With Gratitude and Expectation

I go forth this day in overflowing gratitude for
all the good that is now happening in my life,
repeating my attainment affirmation frequently
and expecting my miracles to happen today
and everyday.

14

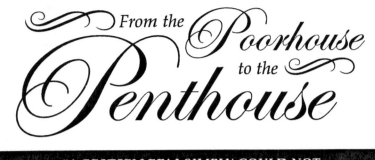

From the Poorhouse to the Penthouse

PRESS RELEASE
By Karen Seaborn
Special for USA TODAY

If you have enjoyed the past favorites: *Think and Grow Rich, The Power of Positive Thinking,* and the recent bestsellers *Who Moved My Cheese, Celestine Prophesies* and *The Prayer of Jabez,* you are going to love, *From the Poorhouse to the Penthouse.*

This easy read catapults your chances for success to the next level, taking you beyond positive thinking into the tangible and proven possibility for limitless, instantaneous success in your finances, weight, health, sales, business and personal life.

The author shares, in one of the most phenomenal success stories ever told, how she literally *believed* her way out of poverty, cancer, depression and obesity—into a multi-million dollar lifestyle of luxury, quick weight loss, and glowing, cancer-free health. Effortlessly attaining everything on a long list in ways and time that go beyond reason and coincidence.

Have you been looking for a way to get your finances in order, improve your life, get out of debt, build your business, lose weight and make more money? Then get this book, because it delivers.

Printed in the United States
38920LVS00005B/181-252